the Taxman!

the Taxman!

EASY WAYS TO SAVE TAX
IN YOUR SMALL BUSINESS

STEPHEN THOMPSON, CA

WILKINSON & COMPANY

CHARTERED ACCOUNTANTS

JOHN WILEY & SONS

Toronto • New York • Chichester • Weinheim • Brisbane • Singapore

John Wiley & Sons Canada, Ltd
22 Worcester Road, Etobicoke, Ontario, M9W 1L1

Canadian Cataloguing in Publication Data

Thompson, Stephen (Stephen Douglas)
  Beat the taxman: easy ways to save tax in your small business

Includes index.
ISBN 0-471-64207-X

1. Small businesses – Taxation – Canada – Popular works.
2. Tax planning – Canada – Popular works.
I. Title.

HJ4662.A3T46 1997   343.7105'26   C96–932374–3

Production Credits
Cover & Text Design: JAQ
Cover Illustration: Dave Anderson
Author Photo: D. Lyle Webb, MPA, Trenton, Ontario
Printer: Trigraphic
Printed and bound in Canada

10 9 8 7 6 5 4 3 2 1

Contents

Round 5 – To Incorporate or Not? A Taxing Question, **49**

Round 6 – GST: Friend or Foe? **61**

Round 7 – 365 Days To Save, 81

Preface

*B*eat the Taxman had its beginnings about three years ago in the form of a "Lunch and Learn" seminar that we created for our clients. The seminars focused on easy tax-planning ideas for the individual investor and businessperson. Several of the ideas discussed in this book originated in those seminars. The main philosophy of the seminars also became the main philosophy of this book: That saving tax dollars involves doing a lot of little things right, throughout the year.

While it's true that under the right circumstances significant tax dollars can be saved using complex structures and high-level tax plans. It is also important to realize that really effective tax planning starts with knowing the rules and doing a lot of little things correctly throughout the year. Tax planning doesn't occur on April 30 when you file your tax return. It occurs when you're planning to purchase that new vehicle, when you're paying your teenage son or daughter that monthly allowance, and when you're recording the revenue and expenses of the business. Tax planning is truly a 365-day-a-year fight. And this book is meant to help you win that fight.

In this book, tax savings is definitely the name of the game. My focus from the outset has been on how I can save you tax dollars. In order to accomplish this task, I have had to explain some of the tax legislation so that I can show you how to use it to your advantage. However, I have intentionally kept the tax explanations short, to the point, and not too complex. My objective is to save you tax, not teach you tax law.

I have also structured the book in an easy-to-understand question-and-answer format. This will allow you to quickly go to a section that relates to your business. For the most part, the chapters of the book, or what I refer to as "Rounds," stand alone. That is to say, you do not have to read the book from start to finish in the order that I have laid out. If a section does not relate to your business, you can skip that section and move on. Where the rules interrelate I refer you to the sections where they are explained in more detail.

I do, however, recommend at least a cursory review of the sections of the book which you believe do not relate to your business. My experience has been that many taxpayers believe certain legislation does not relate to them until they obtain more information. You can save taxes by knowing the rules and acting on them.

Throughout the book I have highlighted important tax-planning ideas by summarizing them in the margins as "Tax Beaters." In the body of the text that runs beside the Tax Beat-

Tax Beater

Deduct the cost of this book and save.

ers, I have explained in more detail how to use the technique to save tax dollars. For example, if you are in business or you are in receipt of commission income, you can deduct the cost of this book as a business expense. If you are in the highest personal income tax level of about 50%, this idea will save you approximately $10. As well, if your business is registered for GST, you will be eligible for an input tax credit of approximately $1.40 on the purchase of this book. This is a savings of approximately $11.40 depending on your province and tax level. In this way I have tried to make tax savings easy and time effective.

For quick reference I have placed at the end the book a summary of all 129 Tax Beaters.

Some Words of Caution

It is impossible to predict every potential tax situation and include it in this book. And, as I mentioned earlier, my focus is on tax savings, not on tax education. I have made a concerted effort to provide an accurate summary of what I consider to be the more important areas in the tax law that was in effect at the time of writing this book, and as that law relates to small and home-based businesses. Many of the ideas in this book are very straightforward. However, there are several areas that are more complex and for which you may need assistance. You should always consider seeking the advice of an expert to ensure that a tax saving idea is right for you. This book is not intended to be a substitute for good professional tax advice.

It is also important to realize that what may make perfectly good sense from an income tax savings point-of-view, may make little sense when reviewed in your particular business situation. I have concentrated on ways to use the income tax legislation to your advantage. However, it is important for you to decide if the ideas make sense in your business. This is a personal assessment which only you can make.

Acknowledgements

This book would not have occurred without the assistance and support of my partners and the staff of Wilkinson & Company, Chartered Accountants. The encouragement and assistance I received is greatly appreciated.

I would especially like to thank Jerry Silverthorn, CA, and Bob Robertson, CA, for their insightful comments and suggestions.

I would also like to thank Steve Klein of Careerwise Inc. His inspiration, ideas, and suggestions were instrumental in making this project happen.

Lastly, I would like to thank my wife Lisa, for her continued, unwavering support and understanding.

Get Off to a Good Start

As with many things in life, starting off right in business can often make the difference between winning the match or getting knocked out after the first bell. Knowing where you stand with Revenue Canada and what the ground rules are going to be can pay dividends to you down the road. In this round, we will look at some of the key questions that are often asked when starting up a new business and how to turn these questions into tax-saving ideas.

What Is a Business?

What is a business? This seems like a pretty straightforward question, one hardly worth spending any time on at all. But, in fact, it is absolutely the first question to ask when you're starting up, and essential for getting started on the right foot.

You may find this statement surprising, but I have found that Revenue Canada and the typical Canadian taxpayer do not always agree! A key area of disagreement concerns the question "What is a business?" Revenue Canada considers a business to be any activity that you conduct for a profit or a reasonable expectation of a profit. The phrase "reasonable expectation of a profit" is the sticky point.

Some entrepreneurs operate what they consider to be a business. But when the business is reviewed honestly and with hindsight, there may have been no reasonable expectation of profit. And in the eyes of the government, without a profit there is no business.

This is not to say that simply because your business is not profitable and eventually fails, the business losses are not deductible. If there was a genuine expectation of profit, then even failed businesses will be considered a business and the losses deductible. However, if you start up your ceramics business and your only customers are your immediate family, and you have no intention of selling your products to make a profit, then maybe you are not operating a business, but simply conducting a hobby.

In most cases, if you are starting out on a new business venture and you honestly believe that in the relatively short term, say within five years, you will be showing a profit, then you are most likely operating a business.

What Is a "Reasonable Expectation of Profit"?

Tax Beater

Report all legitimate business expenses even if you incur persistent losses.

This is a daunting term. It is vague in its definition and vague in its application by both Revenue Canada and the courts. Reasonable expectation of profit is Revenue Canada's ace in the hole. If you are operating a business that is incurring successive business losses, Revenue Canada may try to deny the deduction of your losses by stating that there is no reasonable expectation of profit and therefore no business from a tax point of view. If there is no business, then you cannot deduct your business losses.

Sometimes legitimate business operators fear that if they claim too great a loss or if they have too many years in a row with losses, that Revenue Canada will disallow the deduction of the loss. Some even fail to deduct expenses to increase the loss or, even worse, generate income and pay tax on it to show an expectation of profit. This type of "tax planning" is totally unwarranted and won't solve the problem. If you are operating a legitimate business and believe you have a reasonable expectation of profit, always deduct all legitimate business expenses to reduce your tax liability. If challenged, with a good tax coach in your corner, you can often successfully argue your case and, by obtaining a favourable ruling, "Beat the Taxman."

When Did My Business Start?

In order to maximize your tax savings when starting a business, it is important to know when your business began. For example, did your business start when you made your first sale, or met with your first customer? Or did your business begin when you opened your new bank account, installed the separate telephone line, or purchased your first supplies?

Tax Beater

Record all business-related expenses between startup and your first sale.

It can often be months after this start-up date before sales finally start happening. If you consider your business to have started only after your first sale, then you may lose out on some significant tax deductions.

There are no hard and fast rules on when a business starts. The beginning date is very much dependent on the facts of each particular case. Generally speaking, a business is considered to commence whenever some significant activity is started which is important for the operation of the business. For example, a business may be considered to have started when you begin applying for a licence necessary to operate your business, or when you make your first purchase of supplies or products to sell.

Tax Beater

Don't spend money on your business before official startup.

Any expenses made before the start of a business will not be tax deductible. So before you incur significant costs relating to your business, perform some event which will signify the beginning of your operation. This event may be the registering of your business name with the province or the Chamber of Commerce, or opening up a separate bank account. Whatever it is, do something that signifies the start of operations.

What Types of Expenses Can I Deduct?

Tax Beater

The general rule: All reasonable business-related expenses are tax deductible.

Generally speaking, any reasonable expense that relates to your business is tax deductible. From this basic rule, there are numerous restrictions which the government has legislated to reduce the tax deductions. These restrictions are discussed throughout the book. By knowing these restrictions you can plan around them and maximize your tax deductions.

Am I Really Self-Employed or Still an Employee?

This is an important distinction. If you think you are self-employed but Revenue Canada later decides you are still an employee, then all of the expenses you have tried to deduct may be denied. In many cases it is obvious that you are self-employed: you have several different customers, you are your own boss, you supply your own tools, and you have the risk of losing money.

However, there are many cases where this distinction is much more blurred. In today's world of downsizing, many employers are laying off their staff and hiring contract workers. In many cases, an employee is given a retirement package and then asked to come back on a contract basis. If this has happened to you, are you an employee or self-employed?

The distinction between being an employee and being self-employed is based on the facts of each case. Over the years the courts have developed four tests that they use to determine if you are an employee or self-employed. These tests are:

1. The control test
2. The integration or organization test
3. The economic reality test
4. The specific results test

Tax Beater

Know and follow the rules for self-employment.

The Control Test: If one person holds considerable control over you, in the form of deciding what you will do, how you do it and when you do it, then they may be considered to be your employer. If, on the other hand, you have the liberty to perform the task as you choose, provided it is done within an agreed-upon time, then you may pass this test.

The Integration or Organization Test: This test looks at whether or not you become an integral part of an organization. If your work is so closely tied to your customer's business that you act like any other employee, then you may also be considered to be an employee.

The Economic Reality Test: This is often the most clear-cut test. It looks at whether or not you own your own tools, have a chance to make a profit, or could be at risk of incurring a loss. Where an individual supplies no funds or tools, takes no financial risks and has no liability, the courts have considered the relationship to be employee and employer.

The Specific Results Test: This last test looks at whether or not you are performing a specific task with a distinct completion or whether your services are provided over an extended time frame, with no specific result contemplated. An employee is typically hired to perform various tasks as required on an ongoing basis. A self-employed person would be hired to perform a specific task, the completion of which would end the relationship.

As you can see, these rules are complex and you may require the assistance of a professional. The point is that knowing these rules allows you to arrange your business affairs to ensure you are considered self-employed. Being self-employed will allow you to deduct all legitimate business expenses from the start-up date of your business and will help you win Round 1.

Keep Accurate Records— and Save!

The most often overlooked opportunity to save taxes is keeping adequate business records. I have seen many taxpayers pay excessive taxes simply because they did not create a system that allowed them to keep track of and record all of their business expenses. This round will look at how an effective record-keeping system will help you "Beat the Taxman."

Why Should I Take the Time to Keep Records?

You can save taxes. (Doesn't that make the tedium worth it?)

Most small-business entrepreneurs don't like to spend the time to record their business transactions. It distracts them from what they believe really makes them money, their business. However, I believe that an effective record-keeping system can also make you money, by saving you tax dollars. Good records help to ensure that you are

Tax Beater

Record all expenses to save tax dollars.

reporting all expenses that relate to your business. This will save tax dollars when you do your tax return.

Record-keeping doesn't have to take a lot of your time; the key to an effective record-keeping system is to keep it simple. Whether you use a computer or record your transactions manually, you want the process to be quick and easy. You want a system where you can record all revenue and expenses, but you don't have to spend most of the day doing bookkeeping. When your business becomes more complicated, your record-keeping system can become more complex. But until then, keep it simple.

You can avoid hassles with Revenue Canada. (Definitely worth it!)

Another reason for keeping records is that Revenue Canada says you must. This works for them, but it also works for you.

Tax Beater

Accurate records can help you prove your case to Revenue Canada.

By keeping accurate records you can protect yourself. In criminal law, you're considered innocent until proven guilty. If you've done something wrong, the authorities must prove it. However, with tax law, if there is a dispute, you're normally considered guilty until you can prove your innocence.

The reason for this "reverse judgement" is that the income tax system is self-assessing. You tell Revenue Canada what your income is and they, for the most part, accept this declaration. If they decide to check your return and challenge you on any of your deductions, it is up to you to prove to them that all of your revenue is recorded and that all of your expenses are legitimate. The best way to prove this is to produce the records of your business, complete with bank statements and original invoices.

If you cannot produce any records for Revenue Canada, they are less likely to accept the figures that you have reported on your tax return. Should this occur, you will end up paying considerably more taxes than you originally expected. Therefore, keeping proper records can save you hassles in the long run and, more importantly, can save you tax dollars.

In addition, good records can help to ensure that you are claiming all legitimate expenses. More deductions means less tax and you winning Round 2 with the Taxman.

For How Long Do I Have to Keep My Records?

If you file your income tax returns on time, you must keep your records for a minimum of six years after the end of the year to which they relate. For example, you must keep the records for your 1994 taxation year until the year 2000. You can reduce this six-year requirement if you cease your business operations.

If you file your tax return late, then you must keep your records for six years after the date you filed that tax return. For example, if you filed your 1994 tax return in 1996, then you must keep your records until the year 2002.

If you wish to destroy your records before the minimum time frame is up, then you must get permission from Revenue Canada. To obtain this permission, you can complete form T137 "Request for Destruction of Books and Records" and forward it to your local district taxation office. Alternatively, you can write to the director of your local district taxation office requesting permission to destroy records. This letter must be signed by an authorized representative of your business and should contain the following information:

1. a clear identification of books, records, or other documents to be destroyed;
2. the taxation year for which the request applies;
3. details of any special circumstances which would justify destruction of the books and records at an earlier time than that normally permitted; and
4. any other pertinent information.

What Information Should I Keep?

There are no rules that say precisely what type of records you need to keep. In most cases, the complexity of the business will dictate the complexity of the records. However, as a minimum you should keep the following:

- all original source documents, like invoices and receipts for your expenses
- bank statements, cancelled cheques, and your copy of the bank deposit slip
- your copy of your own invoices and receipts

And, in most cases, you must keep a summary of the year's transactions. This summary could be a simple listing of the various revenue and expense amounts, or it can be a more detailed computerized general ledger produced by one of the many accounting software packages available on the market.

What If I Don't Get a Receipt?

One of the most common reasons why small-business entrepreneurs pay more than their fair share of taxes is because they forget to record all of their expenses. It is easy to forget those expenses when you don't get a receipt.

Even in the cases where you don't get a receipt, you can still deduct the expense. Write in your records the details of the transaction, such as the item purchased, the name and address of the supplier, the date of the transaction, and the amount you paid. This should allow you to get the tax deduction for the expense.

However, whenever possible, try to get a receipt from your supplier. This will help you remember to record the transaction and provide proof of the expense.

Tax Beater

Even without a receipt you can still claim an expense.

What If There Is No Description On a Receipt?

In order for an expense to be deductible, it must be reasonable and it must relate to your business. If your receipts do not indicate what the payment was for, there is no way for you to prove that the expense was for your business.

In most cases, suppliers will provide a description on their invoices. However, sometimes you may receive a cash register receipt that has no description. In this case, write on the receipt a quick description of the purchase. By doing so, you will still be able to deduct the expense in the business.

Tax Beater

Where no description shows on a receipt, itemize the purchase yourself.

How Can I Develop a Simple Record-Keeping System?

Method A: To each its own ... envelope

Recording the transactions for your small business does not have to be complicated. The simplest method for keeping track of your business expenses is to create a separate envelope for each expense and revenue category. For example, if your business is a song-writing and recording studio, expense categories could include "office supplies," "computer and accessories," "advertising," and revenue categories could include "studio rental," "song-writing," and "radio jingle production."

As you incur the expense or receive the revenue, place each receipt in its envelope. At the end of the year, total each envelope and enter the information on your tax return.

This system is very simple and for very small businesses it can be quite adequate. However, if your business is somewhat more complex, this system may not be sufficient to keep track of all of your expenses. This may result in you missing deductions and losing the round with Revenue Canada.

Method B: For wanna-be bookkeepers

A more complicated, yet still relatively simple, system is to combine the method above, of keeping a separate envelope for each expense and revenue category, with recording the transactions. To record your transactions, all you need is some columnar paper. You can buy pads of 14-column paper that are pre-ruled for easy financial record-keeping.

Tax Beater

Record your transactions weekly so you don't forget a business expense.

Along the top of the columns list your major revenue and expense categories. Then, at the end of each week, record each revenue or expense transaction in the proper column. By recording the transactions weekly you are more likely to record all expenses. If you leave the recording of the transactions to the end of the month, you're more likely to forget to record your small purchases.

The advantage with this system is that it is simple and, in cases where there are few transactions, it can be very effective. However, where there are many transactions this system can perform miserably. The main problem is that there is no balancing of the transactions, so you can't check your addition or check your record against your bank account to ensure that all transactions have been recorded. If you have more than 150 transactions a year, consider moving to the next level of record-keeping.

Method C: "Doing the double-entry"

The next level of record-keeping is referred to as the "double-entry" system. With this system you record your transactions in such a way that you can easily tell if you have made an addition error or placed an item in the wrong column. When you are trying to record hundreds of transactions during the year, a misplaced expense in a revenue column can mean hundreds or even thousands of dollars in additional taxes paid to the government. This system prevents such accidents, reduces taxes, and keeps you fighting the Taxman.

With double-entry record-keeping, you should still use envelopes or file folders to keep all of your receipts by major revenue and expense category. Use columnar paper as before, to list each major revenue and expense category across the top of the columns. However, this time, reserve the first three numeric columns for bank deposits, bank withdrawals, and your personal account. Then list your expense and revenue categories. Finally, reserve the last column for miscellaneous expenses.

Now, under the title of each of the columns, write a positive or a negative sign. Bank deposits are a positive, bank withdrawals are a negative. Because your personal account could be either, place a positive and a negative sign. Sales are a negative and all of the expense accounts are a positive. Now you're ready to start recording transactions.

Every transaction you record should equal zero when added across the page. For example, if you were to record a sale of $100, you would enter $100 in the bank deposit column and $100 in the sale column. The bank deposit column is a positive $100 and the sale column is a negative $100; when added together they equal $0.

Here's another example. Say you paid $50 for some business supplies on your personal credit card account, you would enter $50 as a negative in the personal account and $50 under the supplies (expense) account. When these two are added together they equal zero.

Tax Beater

Use a double-entry record-keeping system to avoid costly mistakes.

Date	Description	Bank		Personal	Sales	Supplies	Auto
		Deposits +	Withdrawals −	+/−	−	+	+
Feb 5	Sale—Mr. Brown	100 —			100 —		
Feb 5	ABC Stationary			<50 —>		50 —	

If you are unsure about an entry, try a little trick I use. Always start with the side of the entry you're sure about. With the personal credit card entry, you know you want to add $50 to the supplies account, so enter it on the record. Now you need a negative to get the line to balance and you know the money did not come from the business bank account, it came from your personal account. So the negative must go in the personal account column as a negative.

The double-entry record-keeping system is much more effective in keeping track of all of your business expenses. It is less likely that addition errors will go unnoticed and much more likely that all expenses will be recorded. This process can also be placed on the computer using a simple spreadsheet.

How Do I Know If I Made Money?

So you've been diligent and have been recording all of your transactions throughout the year. Now you want to know if you made any money! An easy way to see how much money you made is to complete the income schedule provided in the Appendix, which is set up under the same format as the information requested by Revenue Canada on their form T2124, "Statement of Business Activities." This government form is used by sole proprietors or partners to report their business income on their personal tax returns.

From your records, add up all of your revenue columns and insert them on the income line. If you have inventory, enter your opening inventory amount, add to that the amount of your purchases. Now subtract your closing inventory. This will provide you with a cost of goods sold figure. Next insert all of your expenses. If you have capital assets, calculate the proper depreciation amount as discussed in Round 9.

Finally, subtract from revenue the cost of goods sold, your expenses, and the depreciation. You can perform this exercise every month using this format to see how your business is doing.

Can I Use the Cash Method for Reporting Business Income?

In most cases, you will not be able to use the cash method for reporting business income. The exceptions are if you are a self-employed commission sales agent or a fisherman or farmer. In all other cases you will have to use the accrual method for reporting business income.

What Is the Cash Accounting Method?

The cash accounting method for reporting business income allows a limited number of taxpayers to report income in the year they receive it and deduct expenses in the year they pay them. For example, if you sold a product but have not received the cash, you don't have to report the income. Once you receive the cash, then you report the sale. With this method you only include in income cash received during the year and you only record as an expense purchases paid during the year.

The cash method is a simple way of keeping track of your income and in many cases can provide an opportunity to legally manipulate your profit. By making purchases at the end of the year and claiming the expense, you reduce income and you reduce your current year's tax liability. But beware, this is often a one-time deferral and once you have started this process, you will find yourself having to continue making purchases at the end of each year to delay the receipt of income.

Tax Beater

By timing purchases and sales at year-end, the cash method can save you tax.

EXAMPLE OF DEFERRING INCOME UNDER THE CASH ACCOUNTING METHOD

First let's assume the following:

	Year 1	Year 2
Sales	$50,000	$50,000
Other expenses	(20,000)	(20,000)
Thus, your profit:	$30,000	$30,000

Now let's assume that at the end of Year 1 you decide you will purchase all of next year's supplies this year. What happens?

	Year 1	Year 2
Sales	$50,000	$50,000
Other expenses including supplies	(20,000)	(20,000)
Adjustment for Year 2 supplies purchased in Year 1	(2,000)	2,000
Total Expense	(22,000)	(18,000)
Net Profit	$28,000	$32,000

In the example, since you purchased Year 2 supplies in Year 1, "other expenses" in Year 2 is reduced by $2,000 because no supplies were purchased. To avoid this income inclusion, you need to purchase Year 3 supplies in Year 2. This will reduce Year 2 profit to $30,000. As can be seen, if you want to avoid the catch-up in one year, once you start prepaying expenses or delaying revenue, you will need to keep doing it into the future.

What Is the Accrual Accounting Method?

Accrual accounting sounds menacing, a term to be used only by professionals for the purpose of keeping their trade a secret. But really, accrual accounting is not complicated. The main principle behind accrual accounting is matching—making sure that revenues are reported in the same year as their related expenses.

For example, say you received an order to perform a service for a customer and you purchased the supplies and conducted the service before the year-end of your business. You billed your customer in the current year but they did not pay your bill until the next year. You have done everything relating to that sale except collect the money. To match the revenue with the expenses, accrual accounting tells us to record the revenue in the current year when it was earned and not in the second year, the year the money was received.

If you were to record the revenue on the sale in the next year when you received the money, you would have the expense in one year and the revenue in the next. The expense would not be matched with the revenue.

The same principle works in reverse. At the end of the year you purchase an item on credit from your supplier. You in turn sell the item and collect the money before the end of the year. Accrual accounting tells us to record the expense of purchasing that item in the current year even though you have not paid for it yet. You match the expense with the revenue.

From this, two general rules can be developed that will assist you in recording your business transactions:

Rule 1: Report the income of the business when it is earned, regardless of when you receive it.

Rule 2: Report the expenses of the business when they are incurred, regardless of when you actually pay the expense.

Do I Have to Use Accrual Accounting Throughout the Year?

The simplest method of recording the transactions of your business is by using the cash basis. Report the transactions of your business as you receive the money or pay the expense. And provided you are not relying on monthly financial statements and your operations are relatively small, I recommend that you record your transactions this way throughout the year.

However, Revenue Canada will require that you report your income on the accrual basis, unless you meet one of the exceptions mentioned on page 15. So, at the end of the year make an adjustment to your records to make them conform with accrual accounting principles.

The typical adjustments required to convert your cash basis records to accrual basis would be as follows:

Start with your income as reported under the cash basis

+ add to this the amount your customers still owed you at the end of the year

− subtract from this the amount your customers still owed you at the end of last year

− subtract from this the purchases which were made during the year but have not yet been paid for

+ add to this the purchases which were made last year but were not paid for at the end of last year

+ add to this the value of your inventory of goods on hand at the end of the year

− and finally subtract from this the value of your inventory of goods on hand at the end of last year

EXAMPLE OF CONVERTING A CASH-BASED RECORD-KEEPING SYSTEM TO AN ACCRUAL-BASED SYSTEM

Income		$40,000
Add current accounts receivable	+	2,000
Subtract last year's accounts receivable	−	1,400
Subtract current accounts payable	−	2,500
Add last year's accounts payable	+	1,200
Add this year's inventory value	+	10,000
Subtract last year's inventory value	−	9,000
Accrual Income		$40,300

These are the most common adjustments for converting your cash-based accounting system to an accrual-based accounting system for small businesses. Depending on your operations, other adjustments may be required.

This procedure will create an accrual basis income or loss figure. From this you will then need to deduct such things as home-office expenses (see Round 8) and Capital Cost Allowance (see Round 9). This will then provide you with the income figure to be reported on your tax return.

Start
With the End
in Mind

Choosing a year-end for your business was once an easy task. Generally, if your business was profitable, a January or February year-end was usually chosen to defer income and the payment of taxes for one year. If your business was losing money, a November or December year-end was preferred to speed up the deduction of your losses.

On February 27, 1995, the government put an end to that planning. In their February budget and subsequent amendments, the government reduced or eliminated the advantages of a non-December year-end. This round will look at how this legislation affects you if you are choosing a year-end. Tax savings are still possible but the rules are complicated and you may have to rely on your tax coach if you hope to win Round 3 and "Beat the Taxman."

Must I Have a December Year-End?

Unless you are in a partnership and one of your partners is another partnership, or worse still if your partnership has an interest in another partnership (I warned you this was complicated), then you still have the choice of having a non-December year-end. If you choose a non-December year-end you must file an election with your personal income tax return.

Why Would I Want a Non-December Year-End?

Tax savings! Tax savings! Tax savings! If your business is profitable, a non-December year-end can still provide you with tax savings by deferring income into the future. Tax deferrals are available in years where the income from your business is increasing. For this reason it may make sense for you to file the prescribed elections and choose a non-December year-end.

Should I Have a December or a Non-December Year-End?

Whether or not you should operate your business with a December year-end or some other year-end is an individual decision which only you can make with some assistance from your tax coach. However, here are some factors you may want to consider:

- If your are just starting a new business and it is losing money, you may want to pick a December year-end to speed up the claiming of the losses which can be used to reduce the tax you will pay on other sources of income.

Tax Beater

Defer tax by staying with a non-December year-end if your income is increasing.

- Generally, if your ongoing business is growing and the income that you are reporting on your tax return is increasing, a non-December year-end will provide a small tax deferral. For example, if your year-end is January, you will include in income an amount prorated based on your January income. If your income is increasing, you will always report a lesser amount with a January year-end than with a December year-end.

- Generally, if your ongoing business is in decline and the income that you are reporting on your tax return is decreasing, switching to a December year-end will save you tax dollars. By having a non-December year-end when your income is dropping, you will be in effect prepaying tax. Switching to a December year-end will stop this from occurring.

Tax Beater

Save tax by changing to a December year-end if income from an established business is decreasing.

- Once you change or start to report on a December year-end basis, you cannot elect back to a non-December year-end. So if you decide you are going to go to a December year-end, make sure that this is the right decision for you, as there is no going back.

- When starting out in a business, if you have significant income from other sources and the business income would be taxed at the highest rate in the first year, consider a non-December year-end to defer the tax liability for a year. However, make sure you plan for the taxes that will become due.

- Overall, December year-ends provide the fewest hassles and frustrations. Having a non-December year-end creates many complexities. If there is very little tax benefit to having a non-December year-end, moving to December is usually in your best interest.

What Happens If I Elect to Have a Non-December Year-End?

If you elect to keep a January year-end, for example, you can continue to complete the year-end of your business for accounting purposes on a February to January basis. However, for tax purposes you will be required to mathematically convert your January year-end to a December year-end.

The conversion to a December year-end is done by multiplying your January year-end profit by the number of days remaining in the calendar year that you operated your business divided by the total number of days in the fiscal year you operated your business. The result of this calculation is then added to your January year-end profit and last year's calculation is subtracted, to give an estimated December profit figure.

For example, assume that your January year-end profit was $50,000. To arrive at your deemed December year-end profit figure you would multiply the $50,000 by 334 days remaining in the calendar year divided by 365 days in the fiscal year of your business. This works out to $45,753. You add the $45,753 to the $50,000 January year-end profit and then subtract the similar calculation that was done in the prior year. If in the prior year your January profit figure was $40,000, then you subtract $36,603 ($40,000 x 334 days ÷ 365 days). The result is that the income you include on your tax return is not the $50,000 your business earned up until January, but instead $59,150 ($50,000 + $45,753 – $36,603).

What If This Is My First Year in Business?

If this is your first year in business and you decide to have a non-December year-end, you may be faced with some very significant cash flow problems if you don't plan properly. In the first year that you report business income, if you have a non-December year-end you must mathematically calculate your income as if you had a December year-end. As described above, if your business had a January year-end and you started your business on February 1 of the previous year, this would mean taking your January profit and multiplying it by 334 days divided by 365 days. However, you would not be able to subtract from this anything for the previous year, as this is the first year of operations. Therefore, in the above example, your income inclusion would be $50,000 plus $45,753 or $95,753.

Remember that the 365 days in the above example represents the number of days in your fiscal year. If, for example, you started your business May 1 and chose a January 31 year-end, the calculation to work out your business income would be $50,000 plus $50,000 x 334 ÷ 276 = $60,507 or $110,507.

By choosing a non-December year-end you have deferred income in the first year, but instead of this deferral continuing for as long as you are in business, as under the old rules, the deferral catches up to you all at once in the next year. If you don't plan for this, you may find yourself having a difficult time paying your tax liability.

Had you picked a December year-end, approximately the same amount of income would have been reported; however, the income would have been spread over two years. With the income being paid over two years, cash flow may be less of a problem and the leveling of the income will make better use of the lower tax rates. Leveling the income out over two years in comparison to having all of the income being reported in one year will save you tax and provide that knockout punch we're all looking for.

The table below shows a comparison of tax payments due on a calendar and a non-calendar year-end assuming a constant $50,000 level of income over three years.

COMPARISON OF TAX PAYMENTS DUE ON A CALENDAR AND NON-CALENDAR YEAR-END

	Calendar Year-End $	Non-Calendar Year-End $
Year 1		
Tax Paid in Year 1	Nil	Nil
Year 2		
April 30 Tax Return Filed for Year 1	16,000	Nil
September 15 Instalment for Year 2	8,000	Nil
December 15 Instalment for Year 2	8,000	Nil
Tax Paid in Year 2	32,000	Nil

	Calendar Year-End	Non-Calendar Year-End
	$	$
Year 3		
March 15 Instalment for Year 3	4,000	Nil
April 30 Tax Return Filed for Year 2	0	39,100
June 15 Instalment for Year 3	4,000	Nil
September 15 Instalment for Year 3	4,000	8,000*
December 15 Instalment for Year 3	4,000	8,000*
Tax Paid in Year 3	16,000	55,100
Total Tax Paid Over Year 1, 2 and 3	48,000	55,100

Assumptions:

- Taxpayer has no other sources of income, is single and living in Ontario
- Taxpayer's income is constant at $50,000 per year
- 1996 rates used

* The taxpayer would elect to make the minimum instalment required expecting that next year's income will be $50,000. (See Round 7.)

How Can I Minimize the Non-December Year-End Tax Problems?

The tax and cash flow problems described above occur because two years of income are included on one year's tax return. To minimize this potential tax problem, the government will allow you to elect to include an amount of income in the first year of operations. This income inclusion can be any amount between zero and the actual business income reported in your first fiscal year times the number of days you carried on business in your first calendar year, divided by the number of days in your first fiscal period.

For example, assume you started your business on March 1, 1996, and you have chosen a January 31, 1997, year end. You have no other income in 1996 and your business income for the period ended January 31, 1997, was $50,000. Your income options for 1996 and 1997 are as follows:

Option 1

In 1996, do not elect to include any business income and therefore pay no tax for your 1996 tax return. In 1997, your income will be $50,000 plus $50,000 times 334 days remaining in the 1997 calendar year divided by 337 days that you operated your business in the first year, or $99,555.

Option 2

You elect to include the maximum amount of business income in 1996. The maximum amount of business income is $50,000 times the number of days you operated your business in 1996, or 306 days, divided by the number of days you operated your business in its first fiscal year, or 337. The maximum amount you would be able to claim on your 1996 tax return would be $45,400.

In 1997, the income you report on your tax return would be the $50,000 plus $49,555 ($50,000 x 334 ÷ 337) minus $45,400 ($50,000 x 306 ÷ 337) or $54,155.

Tax Beater

Elect to include income in your first year of business to reduce income taxed at high tax rates.

Option 3

You elect to include on your 1996 personal tax return business income within the range of zero to $45,400.

This ability to elect an amount to include in income does provide some flexibility in tax planning in the early stages of your business. However, the tax planning is short lived, for whatever you don't include in the first year, you will have to include in income in the second year.

Where this flexibility can be useful, though, is if the excess income is at the same tax level in both years. By electing

Tax Beater

Elect to defer income that will be taxed in the current year at the highest tax rate.

to include in 1996 only enough income to bring your taxable income up to the highest tax level and deferring the balance until next year, you will then provide maximum tax savings and also provide a tax deferral. Deferring the balance into the next year can provide an even greater punch if the tax rates are reducing as they are in Ontario. If the tax rates are increasing, then you may want to re-think this fighting strategy.

When Can I Choose a December Year-End?

At any time, you can switch to a December year-end for your business. By switching, you can avoid all of the hassles and headaches of calculating each year your income inclusion under the non-December year-end format.

Be forewarned, however, that once you switch, there is no turning back. Once you have decided to go with a December year-end and file your tax return in that manner, Revenue Canada will not allow you to later change back to a non-December year-end. So consider talking this over with your tax coach before making the switch.

Who Is Eligible for the Ten-Year Reserve?

In all of the examples used so far, I have not mentioned anything about a reserve. I have shown this additional income being added all in one year. And this is true for anyone who was not in business on December 31, 1994.

If you were in business on December 31, 1994, you may be eligible to claim a ten-year reserve on the additional income that had to be added to your 1995 income tax return. Nineteen-ninety-five was the first year that sole proprietors or individuals in partnerships had to convert their non-December year-end to December.

Whether the individual switched to December as their year-end or chose to keep their non-December year-end, they had to report two years of income in one year. The normal year-end of the business, plus a shortened year-end to December 31. The shortened year-end is often referred to as a stub period income. To provide relief, the government allowed individuals to claim a reserve on the stub period income so that it could be taxed in smaller amounts over ten years rather than all at once. Remember, this ten-year reserve is not available to new businesses or new partners in old partnerships, just businesses and partners that were already in operation on December 31, 1994.

How Does the Ten-Year Reserve Work?

By now, most small-business entrepreneurs that were in business on December 31, 1994, have already filed their 1995 personal tax returns and have, therefore, already gone through the mechanics of how the reserve works. There were a lot of rules, but essentially the reserve allowed you to defer 95% of the stub period income. In 1996, you will be able to defer the lesser of:

1. 85% of the 1995 stub period income,
2. 85% of the 1996 stub period income if you still have a non-December year-end, and
3. the business income for the year.

This will continue with the amount of the reserve dropping by 10% each year until the full amount of the deferred income has been taxed.

Tax Beater

Choose a December year-end if your new business is losing money.

The Tax Rate Stairway: Easy Steps to Saving Money

Understanding how you pay income taxes is key to reducing the amount of tax you pay. In Canada, the income tax system is designed so that, generally, the more money you make, the higher you climb on the tax rate stairway, resulting in more tax that you will pay to the government. This concept is often referred to as the Marginal Tax Rate system, but I like to call it the Tax Rate Stairway, since marginal tax brackets look a lot like stairs in a staircase.

There are four main tax steps or levels. The first tax level has a tax rate of 0%. This rate is applied on income from $0 to the level of your personal tax credit, which for most is $6,456. The second tax level has an approximate tax rate of 27% and is assessed on taxable income between $6,456 and $29,590. The next $30,000 of taxable income, that is income between $29,590 and $59,590, is taxed at a rate of approximately 43%. The balance, or income in excess of $59,590, is taxed at around 50%. Tax rates vary from province to province, with some provinces having a maximum personal tax rate in excess of 53%.

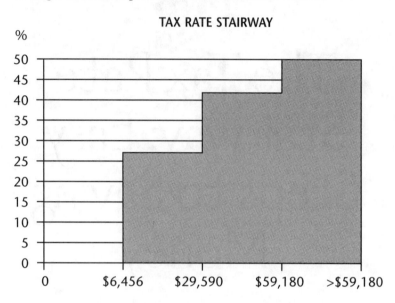

TAX RATE STAIRWAY

How Do I Use the Tax Rate Stairway to Save?

A key to saving taxes is understanding that when your income moves from a lower tax level to a higher tax level, only the increase in income is taxed at the higher rate. For example, say Jane has $30,590 of taxable income. The first $6,456 of taxable income will not be taxed, the next $23,134 will be taxed at about 27%, and the additional $1,000 will be taxed at approximately 43%. Just because Jane has jumped to the third tax level, it doesn't mean that all of her income is taxed at that rate—just the income in excess of $29,590.

Your tax planning objective is to maximize your use of the lower tax levels whenever possible. Poor tax planning occurs when you don't take advantage of the rules that allow you to even out your income from year to year and to avoid those "dreaded" high tax levels.

Tax Beater

Maximize income in lower tax levels and minimize income in higher tax levels.

For example, assume that in Year 1 you have taxable income of $110,000. In Year 2 this drops to $10,000. By averaging your income out to, say, $60,000 for both years, you could save up to $8,500 in tax.

SAVE TAX BY LEVELING YOUR INCOME

	Alt 1	Alt 2
	$	$
Year 1 Taxable Income	110,000	60,000
Year 2 Taxable Income	10,000	60,000
Taxable Income for the 2 Years	120,000	120,000
Tax Paid Over the 2 Years	45,750	37,250
Tax Saved by Leveling Income		**8,500**

Note: Calculations based on no other income, only personal credit claimed and resident in Ontario in 1996. Effects on CPP have been ignored.

What Are the Income-Splitting Techniques?

Now, I recognize that we do not live in a perfect world where we can dictate exactly what our income should be in order to maximize our tax savings. Life should be so easy. But there are many legitimate ways to shift income from one tax level to another. In fact, planning for the transfer of income from one level to another is one of the keys to tax planning.

There are three general techniques for transferring income from a higher tax level to a lower one. The first technique is *Family Income Splitting*. As the name suggests, family income splitting is accomplished by transferring income between family members and maximizing the lower tax levels. This can be done through the use of RRSPs, loans, and salaries.

The second technique is *Personal Income Splitting*. Personal income splitting is accomplished by transferring income from one year to the next on your own personal tax return and maximizing the lower tax levels in the process. This can be accomplished through the use of RRSPs, certain reserves, by applying losses to different years, and by timing discretionary expenses like capital cost allowance.

The third technique is *Corporate Income Splitting.* Corporate income splitting is accomplished by transferring income to a corporation. A corporation is taxed differently than an individual and, sometimes, at a lower tax rate. Maximizing the lower tax rates inside the corporation as well as the family's personal tax rates can result in significant tax savings.

We'll examine each of the three income-splitting techniques in more detail below.

The Family Income-Splitting Technique

The first and easiest technique for effective income-splitting is to split income among your family members. With a small or home-based business, you can do this a number of ways. However, before I discuss the different methods, it is important that you understand "attribution" and how it can foil even the best laid plans.

What Is Attribution?

Recognizing that significant tax savings can be achieved by splitting income among family members, the government has legislated a number of rules to stop people from arbitrarily allocating income between family members. These are known as the attribution rules.

Tax Beater

Save significant tax dollars by legally allocating income among family members.

For example, Mrs. Jones lends money to her spouse to invest and earn investment income. Because her spouse has never worked and has never had a source of income, the investment income earned is attributed back to Mrs. Jones and taxed in her hands at her tax rate. This income-splitting technique is denied because loans made between spouses or minor children for the purpose of investing and earning investment income fall into the attribution rules.

Can I Lend My Spouse Money to Start a Small or Home-Based Business?

One way of avoiding the attribution rules and succeeding in splitting income between family members is a business loan. If you wish to start a business and your spouse has the means to provide you with a loan to help you get started or supplement the operations, then no attribution will occur on the income from the business.

This means that the income earned in the business will be taxed in your hands. The business income will not be added to your spouse's tax return. This result is due to the fact that loans made between spouses or minor children for the purpose of operating a business do not fall into the attribution rules.

Tax Beater

Lending money to a family member to finance a small or home-based business is allowable income splitting.

Can I Pay a Member of My Family a Salary?

An effective method of splitting income with family members is to pay your spouse, child, or parent a salary. A "reasonable" salary paid to your family member will be tax deductible from your business, thereby reducing your tax liability. The salary will be declared as income on your family member's tax return and could be taxed at a much lower level on the tax rate stairway, if it is taxed at all. Be aware, there are restrictions on the salary that you pay to a family member (see "Are There Limits to the Salary I Can Pay to My Family?" on page 36).

Children

Income splitting by paying a teenage child a salary can be extremely advantageous. For example, assume your teenage son or daughter does not have a part-time job but wishes to start saving for post-secondary school or needs money for car insurance, clothing, entertainment, etc. Consider putting them on the payroll rather than just giving them the money.

Tax Beater

Save as much as $3,400 per child, per year, by putting your children on salary.

By putting them on the payroll of your business, you can get a tax deduction for the money you were going to give them anyway, and if the income is less than their personal exemption rate of $6,456, they won't pay any income tax at all. Depending on your circumstances, this could result in an annual tax savings of more than $3,400 per year, per child. It is important to remember that the salary must be reasonable and for work actually performed by your son or daughter.

SAVE TAX BY PAYING YOUR CHILD A SALARY

	Alt 1 (No Salary to Child)	Alt 2 (Salary to Child)
	$	$
Entrepreneur's Taxable Income	80,000	73,600
Child's Taxable Income	0	6,400
Taxable Income for Parent & Child	80,000	80,000
Tax Paid by Both	29,000	25,600
Tax Saved by Paying Your Child a Salary		**3,400**

Note: Calculations based on no other income, only personal credit claimed and resident in Ontario in 1996. Effects on CPP have been ignored.

Parent

Less common, but equally effective, is paying a salary to your parent(s). If their income is low and you wish to assist financially, consider paying them a salary out of your business as opposed to just giving them the money. This can reduce income taxes by providing you with a tax deduction at your higher income tax rate and having it taxed in the hands of your parent at a lower rate. By maximizing the lower tax rates in your family as a whole, you will pay less tax overall. Again, remember the salary must be reasonable for the work performed.

Tax Beater

Pay a dependent parent a salary.

Spouse

Last, but certainly not least, you should consider paying a salary to your spouse. For all the support he or she has provided you, it is the least you can do. However, the savings may not be as great as with a teenage son or daughter.

If your spouse has no other source of income, then you will already be claiming them as a dependant and receiving a tax credit on your tax return for approximately 27% of $5,380. If your taxable income, which includes the income from the business, is $29,590 or less, then there is no tax advantage to pay your spouse a salary. A tax deduction on your tax return at 27% will only be replaced with a tax liability on your spouse's return at 27% or a reduction in the marriage amount at 27%. No real tax advantage is obtained and there may even be a cost with this strategy.

However, if your income is taxed above 27%, then you can achieve real tax savings by paying your spouse a salary. If your business is making, say, $40,000, then paying your spouse a salary of $10,000 can "Beat the Taxman" for $1,500 annually. You can achieve even greater savings if your income is being taxed at the highest tax level. See the chart below for details on how this is calculated.

Tax Beater

If your income is in excess of $29,590 and your spouse is in a lower bracket, pay your spouse a salary.

SAVE TAX BY PAYING YOUR SPOUSE A SALARY

	Alt 1 (No Salary to Spouse) $	Alt 2 (Salary to Spouse) $
Entrepreneur's Taxable Income	40,000	30,000
Spouse's Taxable Income	10,000	20,000
Taxable Income for Couple	50,000	50,000
Tax Paid by Couple	10,930	9,430
Tax Saved by Paying Your Spouse a Salary		**1,500**

Note: Calculations based on no other income, only personal credit claimed and resident in Ontario in 1996. Effects on CPP have been ignored.

The key to this type of planning is to keep in mind the tax rate stairway. Tax savings are obtained from reducing the amount of income that is taxed at high income rates and increasing the amount taxed at lower rates. If both you and your spouse are in the same income tax level, or if your spouse is in a higher income tax level, then it won't make sense to pay them a salary. In these cases, this tax reduction technique is not for you.

Are There Limits to the Salary I Can Pay to My Family?

It is very important to recognize that the salary paid must be reasonable in the circumstances. It would not be reasonable to pay your two-year-old child a salary to reduce income taxes unless this child is actually contributing to the operations of your business. Salaries should not be paid out just to reduce income taxes. You should be able to provide business reasons as to why the particular individual deserves a salary, evidence that the individual actually did work, and that the salary paid is an amount that you would normally pay a stranger.

If you do not take care in paying reasonable salaries for services rendered, you will run the risk of having the tax deduction denied. As well, Revenue Canada may assess an additional penalty of taxing the salary in the hands of the family member. This "double taxation" does get applied occasionally by Revenue Canada. In addition, you will be charged interest on the tax liability caused by the denial of the salary.

Tax Beater

Salary for family members must be reasonable and for services rendered.

These penalties are rare in the case of providing salaries to family members. However, they can and have been assessed in cases where taxpayers have become too aggressive in their planning. This is one Round we definitely want to win so remember "reasonable salary for the work performed."

Does My Family Have to Pay Employment Insurance Premiums on Their Salary?

If you pay your spouse or other members of your family a salary, you must make the proper withholdings and remit these withholdings on time. In most cases, the withholdings will include income tax, and the employee's and employer's portion of CPP and EI (Employment Insurance). However, it may be possible to exempt your spouse and/or your family members from EI. (EI, or employment insurance, used to be known as UI, or unemployment insurance.)

Under the general rules only the owner of a business is exempt from EI. As an owner of a sole proprietorship, all of the profit or loss is yours to report as income or loss on your tax return. None of this profit is subject to contributions to the Employment Insurance plan.

With a corporation, any shareholder who owns more than 40% of the voting shares of the company can be exempt from having to pay EI. So, if your business is incorporated and you own 100% of the shares, you will not have to pay EI on any salary paid to you out of the company.

However, if you hire your spouse, either within an incorporated business or in a sole proprietorship, normally you will have to withhold EI from his or her pay. This would also apply to a salary paid to any other family member.

You can be exempt from paying EI on a family member's salary if the family member acts less as a regular employee and more like an owner of the business. Since your family members are related to you, if their activities in the business resemble those of an owner, family members can be exempt from paying EI and the business will not have to pay the employer's portion.

The logic here is that the government will not pay EI to family members who are laid off if they acted more like owners of the business than merely employees. This is evaluated on a case-by-case basis, with Revenue Canada reviewing each situation to

Tax Beater

Apply to have your family member EI exempt.

Tax Beater

Apply for refunds of EI paid to family members for up to three prior years.

see if the employee would be eligible under the rules to collect EI. If they would not be eligible to collect EI, there is no sense in paying into the plan. Accordingly, you can apply to have your family members exempted.

If you have been paying EI for your family members over the past number of years, you can request a refund of the EI for the past three years. To apply for this refund, ask Revenue Canada for the form PD24(E), "Statement of Overpayment and Application For Refund of Employer's Contribution Under the Canada Pension Plan and/or Premiums Under The Unemployment Insurance Act." Complete this form and submit it along with an explanation of why you feel your family member performs his or her job more as an owner in the business than as an employee.

Revenue Canada will review the PD24(E) form and the reasons for the request and provide you with their ruling. If accepted, Revenue Canada will refund to the employer the portion of the employment insurance contribution that was paid. Revenue Canada will also automatically amend the employee's personal tax returns for the years requested and refund the EI that was withheld from their pay. In some businesses, this has meant thousands of tax dollars refunded.

What About Making Members of My Family Partners?

Paying a salary to a family member provides the most flexible means of income splitting. If the business is doing well, then it may be possible to adjust the family salaries upwards to maximize the lower tax brackets. On the other hand, if the business in not doing that well, the salaries can be adjusted downward. However, the payment of salaries can be an administrative headache.

If your business does not have other employees, placing family members on the payroll will require you to obtain payroll account numbers and to remit withholding taxes, Canada Pension Plan or Quebec Pension Plan contributions, and possibly Employment Insurance contributions. Additionally, depending on the province and the circumstances, you may need to make Workers Compensation and Employers Health Tax payments. It is for these reasons that you should take care to ensure that you achieve substantial savings with your income splitting technique so that the tax savings outweigh the administrative costs.

A simpler method of income splitting with a family member is to go into partnership with the family member. In this case, both or all of the members of the family are owners of the business; therefore, the payroll issues are eliminated. However, in most cases, the profit or loss from the business must be allocated based on a predetermined arrangement, and it is difficult to reasonably adjust this allocation from year-to-year. (This is discussed in more detail in Round 5, "To Incorporate or Not.") However, in many cases, the partnership structure will provide the income splitting desired without the additional costs and headaches involved in having a payroll.

Tax Beater

If you do not already have employees, consider making your family member(s) partners. This avoids costs and headaches involved in having a payroll.

How Do I Use RRSPs for Family Income-Splitting

RRSPs can also be used as a family income-splitting technique. Spousal contributions can maximize your tax deductions today and defer and transfer income to your spouse to be taxed in your retirement years at his or her lower tax levels.

Spousal contributions work by providing the contributor with a tax deduction on his or her tax return. However, since the contribution was made into a spouse's RRSP plan, the non-contributing spouse will report the RRSP in his or her income when the money is taken out.

If you plan to make use of this technique, be careful. There are several rules and objectives to keep in mind when contributing to spousal RRSPs.

First of all, remember that the objective with spousal contributions is to maximize both your own and your spouse's lower income levels when you retire. So you want to build both your own and your spouse's retirement accounts for maximum benefit. If your spouse is likely to be receiving a pension on retirement then spousal contributions may not be for you. On the other hand, if neither of you is going to receive a company pension, both of your RRSP accounts should grow in equal amounts to maximize the use of lower tax levels when you retire.

You must also remember that you must stop making spousal RRSP contributions for three years before your spouse starts withdrawing the contributions unless one of the following situations applies: the RRSP is transferred into a RRIF and no more than the minimum amount is withdrawn, or you become separated from your spouse. There are also special rules if you or your spouse pass away. If you do not stop making RRSP contributions for three years to any spousal plan before your spouse starts withdrawal, the RRSP withdrawal will be included in your income, not your spouse's. These rules apply even if you make spousal contributions to different plans.

Tax Beater

Make spousal RRSP contributions to save taxes today and tomorrow.

The Personal Income-Splitting Technique

Personal income-splitting is more difficult than family income-splitting. As discussed earlier, what I refer to as the personal income-splitting technique is the transferring of your income from one taxation year to a different year, leveling your personal income in the process. Revenue Canada is reluctant to amend prior years' tax returns to perform what is referred to as retroactive tax planning. So instead of amending prior years' returns to maximize the lower tax levels, you must conduct your affairs in such a way as to maximize these lower levels today and into the future. Although more difficult, with a little bit of careful planning, this can still be done effectively.

Why Would I Not Deduct RRSP Contributions?

One effective method of personal income splitting is to delay the deduction of your RRSP contributions. This method can be effective in years where your income is low. For example, assume that in year one your business is not doing very well and your income is being taxed in the lowest tax level of 27%. However, early indications for next year are that your business will be very profitable and you will have income taxed at 53%. By holding off deducting your RRSP contribution until next year, you can get an additional 26% in tax savings from this deduction.

This tax saving occurs because RRSP contributions are treated as a tax deduction, with the tax savings being based on your tax level. If you are in a 27% tax level, for every dollar you contribute to an RRSP, you will save 27 cents. If you are in a 53% tax level, for every dollar you contribute to an RRSP, you will save 53 cents.

Note that in our example the recommendation is to hold off *deducting* the RRSP contribution on your tax return, not to hold off *making* the contribution. For many reasons you should make an RRSP contribution every year. Remember, income earned on the RRSP is not subject to tax until you withdraw the money. So, you can get up to a 53% tax savings with your contribution plus a tax-free return on the money invested. If your next year's income is expected to be low, simply defer deducting your contribution to a high-income year.

Tax Beater

Hold off deducting your RRSP contribution in a year where your income is low and you expect next year's income to be high.

How Can I Make Money When My Business Lost Money?

OK, you had a bad year, and your business lost money. It happens. Even some of the biggest corporations lose money occasionally. It's nothing to be ashamed of. But don't compound your bad luck by not filing your tax return. Make sure you use your business loss to get money back from the government.

Tax Beater

Claim business losses on your tax return to receive an immediate tax refund or reduce future tax liabilities.

Taxpayers sometimes make the unfortunate mistake of thinking that since they lost money, they will have no taxes to pay and don't bother to complete a tax return. As a result, they end up paying too much tax. Despite all of our good income-splitting ideas, not filing your tax return is a sure way to lose Round 4.

Business losses are one of the most flexible personal income-splitting techniques because you can deduct the losses over any of the past three years or the next seven years.

How Do I Calculate My Loss?

If your business lost money in the current year, you may be able to deduct this from income earned in other tax years. But first, you must calculate your eligible loss.

Your first step is to calculate your business loss and enter it on your tax return. Then add in all of your other sources of income, like investment income, pension income, etc. From this, subtract your eligible deductions from income, like carrying charges.

If, after recording all of this information, the taxable income on your tax return is a negative, you will have a loss that can be used to reduce taxes you have paid or will pay.

Note that just because your business lost money, it does not necessarily mean you have a loss which you can carry-forward or carry-back. You must first deduct your business loss from all other sources of income in the current year before you can carry any balance forward or backward.

How Do I Carry a Loss Back or Forward?

Losses can be carried back three years and carried forward seven years. If you want to carry the loss back to any of the three previous years, you must file an election with your current year's tax return. You need to complete Revenue Canada form T1A, "Request For Loss Carry Back" and submit it with your tax return.

Technically, if you wish to carry a loss back, you must file the T1A form by the filing deadline of your current year's tax return. Administratively, Revenue Canada will usually accept late-filed elections; however, there is no guarantee. To ensure that you save all the tax you are entitled to save, file the election on time.

To Which Years Should I Carry the Loss Back?

Deciding which year to apply the loss against is not a precise science and only time will tell if you've made the right choice. But if you do some proper planning, you can make a significant difference in the amount of your tax refund. Make sure you consider the following:

- If it appears that next year you will also have a loss, then consider carrying the loss back to the third previous year. You will never be able to carry a loss back to that particular year again.
- If you expect that this is the only year for a loss, look over your past three years and allocate the loss over the three years to minimize your income. Keeping in mind that your tax planning objective is to maximize the lower tax levels and minimize the higher tax levels, look over your past three tax returns and allocate enough of the loss to each of the years so that the revised taxable income maximizes the lower tax levels.
- If your income for the past three years has been relatively low and you expect that your income in

Tax Beater

File your loss carry-back election on time in order to get your refund.

Tax Beater

Apply a loss to the third prior taxation year before it is too late.

Tax Beater

Apply a loss over the past three years to minimize higher income levels.

Tax Beater

Carry losses forward if next year's income is expected to be high.

future years will be higher, consider carrying the loss forward instead of applying it to prior tax years. The tax refund may not be as immediate, but if you are expecting income in the higher tax levels, the tax savings may be greater.

What Are Reserves?

A very effective method of saving tax through personal income-splitting is in the use of tax reserves. Tax reserves are legitimate ways of deferring income to a future year. And every time you can defer paying tax you save money.

Are There Any Reserves I Can Claim?

There are several different types of reserves, most only apply to specific industries or transactions. However, one reserve that a small-business entrepreneur is likely to encounter is for *services not rendered* or *goods undelivered*.

Assume that your customer pays you in advance to develop a program for their computer. Since you received the money for the job, you record it as a sale. However, by year-end, you haven't completed the job or delivered the product. Since the service hasn't been rendered or the goods haven't been delivered, you don't have to claim the income in this taxation year. You have effectively deferred revenue to the next year, reduced your tax liability, and scored another point in winning Round 4.

Tax Beater

Claim a reserve for income that has been received but in return for which services have not been rendered or goods have not been shipped.

Another common reserve for small businesses is the *allowance for doubtful accounts* reserve. As discussed in Round 2, Revenue Canada requires most businesses to use the accrual accounting method to report income. With this method, you must add to the business's income amounts that have been billed to your customers but not yet collected. Should you feel that one or more of your customers may not pay their bills, then you can claim a reserve for these doubtful accounts.

Claiming a reserve for doubtful accounts does not mean that you are writing off the account and have given up trying to collect the receivable. It does mean that in your best judgement there is doubt about the collectability of the account. This reserve allows you to pay tax on the income in the year you collect the money, not in the year you have made the sale.

Tax Beater

Claim reserves on questionable receivables.

Should I Claim Capital Cost Allowance?

If you own capital assets that are used in your business, such as an automobile, furniture, or a computer, you may be faced with the question of whether or not to claim capital cost allowance (CCA) or depreciation. The CCA rules allow you to write off over a period of years certain large purchases at rates determined by the government. CCA is also a discretionary expense, which means you can defer the claim in the current year or you can claim any amount up to the maximum allowed by the rules.

Since there is so much flexibility with claiming CCA, it is possible to manipulate your income from year to year. This makes using the CCA rules a good personal income-splitting technique. For example, if your income is low one year, you may want to claim less CCA if you expect your income to be at the highest tax level next year. You may get more dollar for your deduction next year, so it may be worth waiting to make the deduction.

However, be warned: with the exception of some fast write-off assets such as computer software and small tools costing less than $200, you cannot double up your deduction. This means that if you choose not to claim CCA one year, the next year you can't claim CCA for both last year and the current year. Each year you can only claim the maximum CCA for that year.

Tax Beater

Defer claiming CCA on fast write-off assets in low income years to get more dollar for your deduction.

As a general rule, you should claim the maximum CCA you can in the current year. However, if you have lots of loss carry forward or fast write-off assets, you might want to defer claiming CCA in low income years and claim the deduction in high income years to maximize your tax refunds.

The Corporate Income-Splitting Technique

As the name suggests, corporate income-splitting involves maximizing the lower tax levels of a corporation and your family. It is one of the most sophisticated forms of income-splitting, but also one of the most advantageous.

Canadian corporations actively involved in a business, like your small or home-based business, can qualify for a very low rate of tax on the first $200,000 of income. (See Round 5 for more details.) In some provinces, this rate can be as low as 17%. By arranging your affairs so that up to $200,000 is taxed within a corporation, you can defer up to 34% in taxes annually. This can mean an annual tax saving of up to $68,000! This could be Round 4's knockout punch.

Eventually, you will want to take this money out of the corporation. What good are tax savings if you can't spend them. When you do, you may pay another tax on the corporation's payment to you. When you add these two taxes together, they will equal approximately what you would have paid if you had received the money directly, without using a corporation. However, until you need to withdraw that money out of the company, that second level of tax is deferred and you have saved up to $68,000.

You can obtain significant tax savings through the use of a corporation, with tax deferral being the name of the game. However, for all but the most successful small and home-based businesses, the use of a corporation is not necessary. For a corporation to be truly useful, your business needs to be earning enough income to maxi-

Tax Beater

Highly successful small-business entrepreneurs should consider using a corporation to defer up to $68,000 a year in taxes.

mize your family's personal tax rates and you need to be in a position to leave the savings in the corporation. If you meet these criteria, then consider a corporation.

Corporate income-splitting can involve the use of several corporations and/or family trusts. Due to the complexities involved with proper corporate income-splitting, I highly recommend you see your tax coach. When your business becomes successful enough to make use of sophisticated corporate income-splitting techniques, it is time to seek proper professional advice. It may seem expensive, but good professional advice will almost always save you money.

To Incorporate or Not? A Taxing Question

Almost immediately after deciding on what business to start, many entrepreneurs begin thinking about incorporating their businesses. And it's easy to see why. All of the big, successful businesses are corporations. Many of the successful business leaders in your community own and operate businesses that are incorporated. And at cocktail parties everyone is talking about how they own this corporation and that corporation. It makes them appear successful and sophisticated. Owning a corporation can be something of a status symbol. And it's only natural to want to keep up with the Joneses. You're starting a business which you believe will grow and grow and who knows, may become a huge enterprise. But that doesn't mean you should run out now and incorporate. Remember, we want to take every opportunity to "Beat the Taxman." Before we look into whether or not a corporation is right for you, let's first look at what options you have to structure your business.

What Are the Common Business Structures That I Can Use?

Tax Beater

Save time and money by choosing the proper business structure.

The *Income Tax Act* accommodates many complex forms of business structures, most of which would not be looked at by small-business owners or home-based entrepreneurs and are beyond the scope of this book. However, there are three business structures that are common and widely used by small and home-based businesses: *sole proprietorship*, *partnership*, and the *corporation*. Knowing which structure is appropriate for you can save you time and money.

What Is a Sole Proprietorship?

When an individual operates a business and includes the profit or loss of that business on their personal tax return, they are typically considered to be operating as a sole proprietor. There are three characteristics of a sole proprietorship:

1. a single individual owns the business
2. normally the business is in the individual's name or trade name
3. the profits and losses of the business are reported on the individual's personal tax return.

What Are the Advantages of a Sole Proprietorship?

The main advantage of a sole proprietorship has to be the ease of getting started. It can cost little or nothing to start a business as a sole proprietor. And you can start the business immediately. It can be as simple as just starting to keep receipts or opening a bank account. You can register your business name if you wish to use a trade name like "Joe's Garage" or you can just operate as "Joe's," without registering your business name.

A sole proprietorship is by far the easiest structure to set up, which also makes it the most popular with very small and home-based businesses.

Another benefit with this structure is very little government regulation. With a corporation you must operate within the regulations of the *Canada Business Corporations Act* or the provincial equivalent. A partnership is subject to more tax rules and filing requirements than a sole proprietorship. Overall, the sole proprietorship provides the least government regulation.

The sole proprietor is in control over his or her business and doesn't have to waste time convincing other people that their idea is the right idea.

A last benefit of a sole proprietorship is that all of the profits of the business go to the owner. You won't have to share with anyone the profits of your business. The flip side of this is, of course, that all the losses also go to the owner, which means that you are not sharing the risk of ownership with anyone.

What Are the Disadvantages of a Sole Proprietorship?

The main disadvantage of a sole proprietorship is unlimited liability. Unlimited liability means that you will be personally responsible for all debts and obligations of the business. If your business goes under, you may have to sell personal assets in order to cover the debts of the business.

Another disadvantage of a sole proprietorship is that once the owner passes away or loses interest in the business, the business ceases to operate. With a corporation, the business can live on despite the fact that the owner of the shares retires or dies.

A third disadvantage is that it can often be difficult to raise capital. As a sole proprietor you are the only one responsible for raising money for the business. You don't have partners or investors to help you out financially. However, if you don't need much financing, this isn't much of a concern.

One last disadvantage of being a sole proprietor is the possible perception by fellow business owners that you are unsophisticated. As discussed previously, many people unfortunately think that you must operate a corporation in order to be successful, and to be a good entrepreneur. However, there are many sole proprietors who are very wealthy and sophisticated and there are many owners of corporations who are not wealthy at all and are in no way sophisticated. A business structure does not in itself dictate your level of sophistication. Only time and success will prove that.

What Is a Partnership?

A partnership is best described as two or more sole proprietors who get together to work as a team in one business. A partnership is like a sole proprietorship in that the profit and losses of the partnership are reported on the partners' individual personal tax returns except that, unlike a sole proprietorship, there are two or more owners of the business.

It is important to realize that the ownership of a partnership does not have to be split evenly between the partners. A partnership can be a 50/50 partnership, a 60/40, a 90/5/5 or any other combination, and still qualify as a partnership. A partner reports his or her share of the business's profits or losses based on the relative percentage of their ownership in the partnership.

What Are the Advantages of a Partnership?

One of the main advantages of a partnership is ease of formation. Just like a sole proprietorship, a partnership can be formed quite easily and with very little cost. You will have to register the name of a partnership with the province, which is not mandatory for a sole proprietor, but other than that, there are few other registrations required.

Another advantage is the ability to turn to your partners for additional sources of financing for the business. It is no longer simply up to you to borrow money. With a partnership, you have more people providing assistance to help keep the business going.

With a partnership, there are more government regulations than for a sole proprietor, but still far fewer than with a corporation. This will normally reduce the amount you have to pay lawyers and accountants.

A partnership also provides an opportunity to combine the skills of the individual partners. Partnerships often form because one individual is a fantastic seller and the other individual has the expertise and interest to oversee the making of the product and the administering of the office. Their combined skills produce a more successful team.

And remember, your assets are not the only ones on the line, you get to share the risks of ownership with your partner.

What Are the Disadvantages of a Partnership?

As with a sole proprietorship, unlimited liability is also the main disadvantage of a partnership. You and your partner will be personally liable for all the debts and obligations of your business.

Another problem is divided authority. How do you resolve differences of opinion? You may have to make compromises which are not necessarily good for the business. As well, it may be difficult to find suitable partners. And what if you find someone you think is a suitable partner, only to find out later it was a bad mistake? How do you ask a part owner to leave?

My advice is to have a partnership agreement signed, sealed, and delivered before you start into business. This legal document spells out how the partnership will work. It will ensure that there is a mechanism in place for dealing with differences of opinion, handling the departure or death of one partner, forced resignations, breakup, and major operating issues. Regardless of the number of partners or the size of your business, drawing up a partnership agreement is the right thing to do.

Tax Beater

To save money and avoid hassles, develop a partnership agreement.

What Is a Corporation?

A corporation is a separate legal entity. Like a separate person, it must file its own federal and provincial tax returns and register itself with either the provincial or federal government.

As a sole proprietor or a partner, the profits and losses of the business were yours and you reported them on your tax return. As an owner, you don't pay yourself a salary or issue yourself a T4, because you will be reporting your share of the profits on your tax return. But the corporation is a separate entity and, as such, all of the profits and losses are reported on the corporation's federal and provincial tax returns. If you wish to report some corporate income on your own personal tax return, you must pay yourself a wage out of that corporation.

What Are the Advantages of a Corporation?

There are two main advantages of using a corporation. The first addresses the major shortcomings of the other two structures. A corporation can provide limited liability. For the most part, the corporate debts are not an obligation of the individual shareholders.

The other main advantage is income tax savings. It is possible to save considerable tax dollars by using a corporation. However, this is not the case in all circumstances. How you can "Beat the Taxman" with a corporation will be discussed later in this round.

What Are the Disadvantages of a Corporation?

A significant disadvantage of using a corporation is the increased amount of government regulation and the associated costs. If you wish to use a corporation, you must incorporate a company, which can cost you from $300 to $1,500, depending on the complexity of the corporate structure and whether or not you use a lawyer. You will have to complete separate tax returns and financial statements for the corporation resulting in more than doubling the number of tax returns you have to file.

With the added complexity of corporate tax returns, it becomes even more important to solicit the assistance of a tax coach. More tax returns and greater complexity means more professional advice and costs. Under the right circumstances, this is fine. If your business is successful, then the fees you will pay for good advice should outweigh the costs, but the conditions have to be right.

This leads us into the last main disadvantage of a corporation. Sometimes there can actually be a tax cost to using a corporation. With a sole proprietorship or partnership, if your business incurs losses, especially in the start-up years, these losses can be deducted against other sources of income. You can deduct the losses against your pension income, your interest income, or that part-time job you have to pay the bills. If the loss is really substantial, resulting in a taxable loss overall on your tax return, then this loss can be carried back three years and forward seven years to deduct against other sources of income. This is a real advantage of sole proprietorships and partnerships.

Tax Beater

Save taxes in start-up years where you have losses by using the sole proprietorship or partnership structure.

With a corporation, since it is a separate legal entity, the losses cannot be applied against income on your personal tax return. Instead, the losses can only be deducted against income within that corporation. The losses can be carried back three years and forward seven years, but have to remain in the corporation. This is a significant drawback of a corporation when times are tough.

What Tax Savings Can Be Achieved By Using a Corporation?

There are two key objectives in tax planning. The first is to save overall tax dollars; you want to reduce, in absolute terms, the tax that you have to pay. The second and equally important objective is to defer for as long as possible the payment of this tax. By delaying the payment, you, in effect, save money. You now have more money for your business. A corporation is an effective tool in helping with the second objective, deferring the payment of tax dollars.

With a corporation, income is broken down into two main classifications, specified investment income, sometimes referred to as passive income, and active business income. Passive income is income you receive from such things as investments in the stock market, long term GICs, term deposits, bonds, etc. It is income that is generated automatically, or passively, from an investment.

Active business income is income you receive from business operations. As a small-business entrepreneur, most or all of your business income will be considered active business income. This distinction is important because the *Income Tax Act* taxes the two types of incomes differently. The first $200,000 of active business income earned inside a corporation owned by a Canadian resident is taxed at only about 22% (the actual tax rate will vary depending on your province). Passive income, on the other hand, is taxed at a rate slightly greater than 50% (again depending on the province). A significant difference.

However, as a small-business entrepreneur, all, or substantially all, of your income will likely be considered active business income and, therefore, will be taxed at the lower rate. The tax deferral works by making use of this lower tax rate inside the corporation. But in order for the tax planning to be really effective, we must also maximize the lower tax brackets at the personal level.

Sounds complicated? Well, let's see how it works. Assume for a moment that your company made $100,000. You then pay yourself a salary of $60,000 to maximize the lower tax brackets, leaving $40,000 to be taxed in the corporation. At $60,000 in personal income, you are at the top of the Tax Rate Stairway, as discussed in Round 4. Any additional salary paid to you at that level will be taxed at 50%. If the income is left in the corporation it will be taxed at about 22%. The difference represents a tax deferral of 28%.

Tax Beater

Defer up to 28% in taxes by using a corporation properly.

This is only a tax deferral since you haven't yet received that $40,000 out of the corporation. In order to get the $40,000 (less the corporate tax you will pay on the $40,000) out of the corporation, you will need to pay yourself a dividend and pay tax personally on the dividend of up to 36%. This rate will vary from province to province and is lower at different levels on the Tax Rate Stairway. The 36% rate being used here is the rate at the highest level on the stairway.

This tax savings then only works if you can leave money in the corporation for a number of years, normally for three to five years. If you need the money for personal reasons and you are constantly removing the cash from the corporation, you will not be able to take advantage of this idea to "Beat the Taxman."

TAX DEFERRAL AVAILABLE BY USING A CORPORATION

Assumption: The individual is at the highest tax level.

Alternative 1—Earned Directly by Individual	**$**
Income Earned by the Individual	40,000
Personal Tax Paid (50%)	(20,000)
Cash in Individual's Hands	20,000

Alternative 2—Earned Through a Corporation	
Income Earned by the Corporation	40,000
Corporate Tax Paid (22%)	(8,800)
Cash Remaining in Corporation	31,200
Tax on Dividend on Distribution of Cash to Shareholder (36%)	(11,200)
Cash in Individual's Hands	20,000
Tax Deferral Available (Tax that can be Delayed on Payment of Dividend)	**11,200**

Note: The $11,200 is not a tax savings but a deferral. The $11,200 tax on the distribution of the dividend is deferred until you actually pay the money out of the corporation, which may not occur for a very long time.

Is There a Tax Advantage to Selling Shares of My Corporation?

Another significant tax advantage you gain by using a corporation is the ability to use the $500,000 capital gains exemption on the sale of the shares. The capital gains exemption received a considerable amount of press and discussion in 1994 and 1995 when the federal government announced in the February 22, 1994 budget the elimination of the $100,000 capital gains exemption. The $100,000 capital gains exemption was available on other property like shares listed on the stock market, mutual funds, and cottage property. (The use of the capital gains exemption on cottage property really ended in 1992.)

But what didn't receive as much press at the time was that the capital gains exemption can still be used on the sale of shares in a qualified small Canadian-owned business or farm property. *And* that this capital gains exemption is $500,000 in value. Talk about "Beating the Taxman." This one idea could save you up to $195,000 in income taxes.

With this in mind, there can be a significant advantage to selling shares of your business rather than selling assets. However, it is often difficult to find a buyer who is willing to purchase shares. There are risks associated with buying someone else's shares and a tax incentive for the buyer to purchase assets. So if you want to sell shares, you will normally have to discount the price, which will start to reduce your tax benefits. And depending on your personal tax returns, you may not be able to make use of the capital gains exemption. The government restricts the use of this exemption in some cases where taxpayers have claimed investment losses.

If you can make use of the exemption and you can structure the deal to be a sale of shares, you can save considerable tax dollars. Be aware however, that this is an extremely complex area of tax legislation. If you're planning to sell your business in the near future,

Tax Beater

Save thousands of dollars by selling shares that qualify for the $500,000 capital gains exemption.

I strongly advise you to seek out a good tax coach to have in your corner. If done incorrectly, the sale of shares could cost you more than if you had just sold assets in a straightforward deal.

So Which Structure Is Best for Me?

Determining which structure is best for you is one of the more difficult decisions you will have to make. Once again the advice of a tax coach can be invaluable.

But in the meantime, here is a good rule of thumb. If you need all the profit that the business is generating to cover living expenses, a corporation is likely not for you. Remember, one of the main advantages of the corporate structure is the ability to defer income by leaving profit in the corporation. If you need all the money generated by your business for personal needs, you won't be able to take advantage of the tax deferral.

The other key advantage to a corporation may be to protect your personal assets in the event of an unforeseen business loss. Earlier, we discussed the concept of limited liability. This means that a corporation's unsecured creditors can take no action against the personal assets of the owner in the event that the corporation does not pay its creditors. Unfortunately, banks and trust companies and many trade suppliers won't loan new corporations money without excellent security and, in most cases, that security can include the owner's personal guarantee. When this happens, the corporation does not protect the owner's personal assets.

However, if you operate a business where the risk of accident or lawsuit is high, for example, a small construction company, a corporation may be useful in providing you additional protection. Generally, you would insure against accidents or lawsuits; however, if the losses from these actions exceeded your insurance coverage, then the corporation would act as a shield in protecting your remaining personal assets.

But if it is unlikely that you are going to be sued for large amounts, if you don't have significant unsecured creditors, and if you are not taking advantage of any of our tax deferral ideas, then more likely a corporation is not for you.

Here's one last thing to think about when trying to decide whether or not you should use a corporation. It is possible to transfer all or any part of a business operating as a sole proprietorship or a partnership into a corporation at any time, tax free. So the best advice usually is to operate as a sole proprietorship or a partnership until your business is established and you can determine if a corporation will be of benefit to you. If you decide that a corporation will provide some tax benefits, roll the business tax free into the corporation at that time. Often the worst tax planning is to start up a business in a corporation that is losing money and you have no way of deducting those losses against personal income. It is better to keep the business outside the corporation until it starts becoming profitable and then transfer it to the corporation.

Tax Beater

Save taxes by transferring profitable businesses into a corporation and keeping losing businesses as sole proprietorships.

ROUND SIX

GST: Friend or Foe?

Despite what some might say, the GST is here to stay. Governments may change the name of the tax, or get other provinces involved, but some form of consumption tax, like the GST, is going to remain a part of our tax structure for some time to come. You just can't replace the revenues that the GST is providing without creating a new tax or increasing the current tax rates. Both alternatives would mean political suicide in the current environment. So, like it or not, the GST is here to stay.

So if the GST is going to stick around for awhile, maybe it's time you look carefully at your business to ensure that you are minimizing the GST you pay on a year-to-year basis. This round will review in general terms how the GST works but, but more importantly, it will highlight what you should know to minimize the GST you pay.

What Is an Input Tax Credit?

An input tax credit is the term used for providing a refund to a business for the GST it pays on its purchases. All businesses that are selling taxable goods and services, and who are registered, are eligible for a refund of the GST that they pay on their purchases. What this means is that for most businesses, the GST is not a tax to them at all. On the one hand, a business charges and collects for the government the GST on its sales. On the other hand, the business will pay GST on its purchases, but the government refunds to the business the GST on these purchases. There is no tax cost to the business from being registered for the GST.

There can, however, be administrative costs associated with keeping track of the GST. The "hassle factor" on the GST can be fairly high. As well, there can be a cost associated with "cash-flowing" the GST, as the government will want their money even if you haven't collected your money from the customer. This makes us ask the question: "is the GST our friend or our foe?" The GST is friendlier to businesses than income taxes and payroll taxes, as it is not a direct cost of doing business. Yet the GST is our enemy when we make those personal purchases which are not eligible for any input tax credit rebate. Friend or foe, it's up to you to decide.

Do I Have to Register for the GST?

You must register for the GST if your sales of taxable goods and services during the fiscal period of your business exceed $30,000. You are required to register and begin charging the GST the month after you reach the $30,000 threshold. You cannot wait until the following year to register.

Most goods and services sold in Canada are taxed at the 7% federal GST rate. Some goods and services however, are taxed at a 0% rate. I recognize that a 0% tax rate appears unusual. You might ask why not just call these goods and services non-taxable goods and services? Well, the distinction of non-taxable goods and services and goods and services taxed at 0% is important.

Tax Beater

Register for GST if you are selling zero-rated goods and services to obtain refund of GST on purchases.

In order to be eligible to claim a refund of GST on your purchases, you must be selling taxable goods and services. Goods and services subject to a tax rate of 0% would still qualify the business for a refund of GST on its purchases since the sales are taxable. Companies that sell goods and services that are non-taxable or exempt from tax are not eligible for a refund of GST on their purchases. This is a very important distinction indeed. Examples of goods and services subject to the 0% tax rate, or what is referred to as zero-rated goods and services, are listed below.

EXAMPLES OF ZERO-RATED GOODS AND SERVICES
- sales of basic groceries (e.g., milk, bread, and vegetables)
- sales of agricultural products, farm livestock, and most fishery products
- sales of prescription drugs and drug dispensing fees
- sales of medical devices (e.g., hearing aids and artificial teeth)
- all exports (goods and services taxable in Canada are zero-rated if exported)

Source: Revenue Canada

If you sell what is referred to as *exempt goods and services*, you will not be required to register at all. Registration is not required since you cannot charge GST on your sales, nor are you eligible to receive a refund of GST on your purchases. GST will, under these circumstances, become a real tax cost to your business. Examples of exempt goods and services that might be common among small business and home-based entrepreneurs are listed below.

EXAMPLES OF EXEMPT GOODS AND SERVICES

- sales of used residential housing
- residential rents of one month or more and residential condominium fees
- most health, medical, and dental services performed by licensed physicians or dentists
- child-care services provided primarily to children 14 years old and younger
- legal aid services
- music lessons
- arranging for and issuing insurance policies by insurance companies, agents, and brokers

Source: Revenue Canada

Should I Register for the GST?

If you are not required to register for the GST, and you sell taxable goods and services, you will be left with the question of whether you should register for the GST voluntarily. This is a difficult question, one that can only be answered by looking at each individual's personal situation. Before you make your decision, here are some issues to think about.

First of all, as a registrant you will be eligible for input tax credits. This means that by registering you will be able to reduce the cost of your purchases subject to GST by 7%. This is a significant reduction in the cost of your operations.

Tax Beater

Register for the GST and increase profits.

Secondly, you will have to start charging GST on sales to your customers. How will this affect you from a competitive point of view? If none of your competitors are charging GST, then maybe you will lose customers if you become registered and start charging GST. If all your competitors are charging GST, registering may allow you to be more competitive, passing on your GST savings to your customers.

Additionally, you need to look at who your major customers are. If most of your customers are businesses that would also be registered for the GST, then they won't care if you're registered or not. The GST won't be a cost to them. And as I noted, since registering reduces your costs, you increase your profits or decrease your prices.

Remember one firm rule: once your taxable sales exceed $30,000 in a taxation year, you are required to register for GST in the following month.

One last factor is that input tax credits can only be claimed from the date of registration. For example, assume you don't register your business for the GST in your first year of operations because your sales will be less than the $30,000 threshold. Assume also that, like many new businesses, you have to purchase some assets to begin operations. For example, you may purchase a van, a computer and software, or office supplies. On all of these purchases, you would have had to pay GST. Yet because you did not register to charge GST on your sales, you will not be allowed to get any of the GST back. You cannot claim an input tax credit for the period before you are registered for the GST. This is one reason why many new small-business entrepreneurs register for the GST immediately.

Tax Beater

Register for the GST at start up and claim input tax credits on all your business purchases.

Can I Simplify the Administration of the GST?

One of the major disadvantages of the GST for businesses is having to keep track of all the GST that you pay and collect. Recording GST in journals can increase significantly the amount of time spent on record-keeping. However, for small businesses there are solutions; in fact, there are two solutions.

In recognizing that recording the GST is a hassle, the government decided to offer two simplified methods to assist in the reporting of the GST for small businesses. The two methods are called the "Simplified Method," used to calculate input tax credits, and the "Quick Method," used to calculate your net GST remittance.

Simplified Method

With the "Simplified Method" you do not have to record separately in your books the GST on your purchases. Normally, if you wish to claim an input tax credit, you would have to go through and add up all of the GST you paid on all of your purchases during the period. If you are keeping a journal, you would keep a separate column reserved for the GST and record in that column the GST that you paid. With the "Simplified Method," you are not required to do this calculation.

Instead, what you would do is simply add up all of your taxable purchases and multiply this number by 7/107. For example, if all of your taxable supplies, including the GST and other non-refundable provincial and other taxes total $2,000, you would be eligible for an input tax credit of $130.84 ($2,000 x 7/107). This method can save time and money.

In order to qualify for the simplified method, taxable sales and taxable purchases in the preceding year can not have exceeded $500,000 and $2 million respectively. If you qualify, just start using this method at the beginning of your fiscal year. If you start using this method, you must stay with it for at least one year, unless you no longer qualify.

The problem with the simplified method is that it still requires you to separate taxable purchases from non-taxable purchases. For example, employee salaries, insurance, interest on loans, and other exempt or zero-rated purchases must be separated from the taxable purchases so you can calculate the input tax credit. For some businesses this is not a problem, and due to the volume of taxable purchases, real savings can be achieved. With other businesses, because they make few purchases, it may be just as easy to separate out the GST. If this method can save you time, consider using it.

Quick Method

If the "Simplified Method" didn't seem easy enough, maybe the "Quick Method" will be more to your liking. The "Quick Method" is truly a simple way to calculate and remit GST. If you can qualify to use this method, all you need to do is collect the GST on your taxable sales and then remit to the government either 2.5% or 5% of the total sales including GST. With this method, you do not calculate or obtain input tax credits on normal business expenses. These input tax credits are replaced with the portion of the 7% sales tax not remitted to the GST office.

For example, if during the past year you had taxable sales of $100,000 including GST, and you qualified for the 5% rate, (see explanation later in this section) then you would have collected $6,542 from your customers (calculated as $100,000 x 7/107). Of this $6,542 that you have collected from your customers, you remit to the government $5,000 ($100,000 x 5%). This leaves you with $1,542 as your input tax credit. If the actual GST paid for the year for which you are eligible for an input tax credit was less than $1,542 then you will be better off using the "Quick Method."

Tax Beater

Reduce tax and simplify GST record-keeping by using the "Quick Method."

If your actual input tax credits would have been greater than the $1,542 in this case, then you will have to weigh the cost of losing eligible input tax credits against the additional time and aggravation of calculating the input tax credit.

To be eligible to use this method, your annual taxable sales including GST must be $200,000 or less. In addition, there are a number of industries that will not qualify under the program. (See the list on page 68.) To start using the "Quick Method," complete GST form 74E, "Simplified Accounting Methods for Small Businesses Election Form" and send it your local Revenue Canada district taxation office.

TYPES OF BUSINESSES NOT ELIGIBLE TO USE "QUICK METHOD"

- accounting
- audit services
- financial consulting
- lawyer or law offices
- insurance
- dealer in financial instruments
- notary public
- tax preparation services
- tax consulting

Source: Revenue Canada

The 5% "Quick Method" rate applies to most small businesses. Examples might include small manufacturers, consulting businesses, delivery businesses, etc. The 2.5% "Quick Method" rate is reserved for retailers and wholesalers. Typically with these types of businesses there are lower profit margins and a very high rate of taxable purchases. Accordingly, the "Quick Method" rate is lower. If you are unsure which rate to use, your local district taxation office can help you.

Tax Beater

Maximize your GST savings by claiming the 1% reduction.

If you elect to use the "Quick Method," keep in mind the 1% reduction in both rates on your first $30,000 of sales. As an incentive to use this method, for the first $30,000 of sales the rates are only 4% and 1.5%. Once your sales, including GST, go over the $30,000 mark, you must start remitting based on 5% or 2.5% as appropriate in your case.

Tax Beater

Remember to claim input tax credits on capital purchases when using the "Quick Method."

If you are using the "Quick Method," make sure you still claim input tax credits on your capital purchases like computers, office equipment, machinery, vehicles, and even software. The "Quick Method" is meant to reduce the administrative burden on everyday business sales and purchases. With the not-so-everyday purchases of vehicles and equipment, you are still eligible to claim an input tax credit. When you sell used capital goods like old computers, your vehicle, etc., then you will also have to remit the GST on the sale, over and above the "Quick Method" calculation.

Can I Still Claim Input Tax Credits If I Forgot to File My GST Return?

If you have registered for the GST, you have up to four years from the day the GST return was due for the period in which the purchase was made to claim your input tax credit on the purchase, provided your taxable sales were less than $6 million and you were not a listed financial institution. For example, assume you must file your GST returns quarterly, and you make a purchase of a $20,000 vehicle, used exclusively in your business, in January, 1996. The GST you paid on the vehicle is $1,400. The year-end of your business is December 31, 1996. You will have until April 30, 2000, to claim that input tax credit.

Tax Beater

Claim forgotten input tax credits before the four-year limitation is up.

With a December year-end, the first quarter of 1996 ends in March. Your GST return is due one month after the end of the quarter. You then have up to four years from that date to claim any forgotten input tax credits. After the four years, you won't be able to apply for the refund.

Can I Be Denied a Legitimate Input Tax Credit?

To claim an input tax credit, you must have invoices or receipts containing certain information. The amount of information varies depending on the invoice amount. The table on page 70 shows what information is required for different invoice amounts.

INFORMATION REQUIRED FOR DIFFERENT INVOICE AMOUNTS

Information Required	Total Purchase Under $30	Total Purchase $30 to $149.99	Total Purchase $150 or more
Your business or trading name	✓	✓	✓
The date of the invoice	✓	✓	✓
The total amount paid or payable	✓	✓	✓
Detail on what is subject to GST and either the total amount of GST charged or a note that the total includes GST		✓	✓
Your GST registration number		✓	✓
The purchaser's name or trading name			✓
Terms of payment			✓
A brief description of the goods or services			✓

Source: Revenue Canada

If a receipt or invoice for a purchase you make does not contain the proper information, the government can deny the input tax credit on the purchase. The key detail that Revenue Canada auditors look for in most cases is the GST registration number. If the purchase is for more than $30 and there is no GST registration number on the purchase invoice or sales receipt, Revenue Canada may deny your input tax credit.

Tax Beater

Request GST information be included on purchase invoices to save money and hassles.

The onus is on you, the purchaser who is claiming an input tax credit, to ensure that all the information is present to substantiate your claim. If you are being charged GST and the invoice you are receiving does not provide the required information, ask for it to be written on the invoice. It could save you hassles and money later on.

Can I Claim an Input Tax Credit on Capital Purchases?

One of the most often forgotten claims for input tax credits relates to the GST paid on capital purchases. This happens because capital purchases are not recorded the same way as normal everyday expenses. It's not every day that you go out and buy a car. So when you record the vehicle in your books, you may forget about the GST you paid. Or when you add up the GST you paid from all your regular, day-to-day invoices, you may forget about that special purchase of a vehicle or computer.

Sometimes, the GST paid on a capital purchase is so large in comparison to your normal activity that it will result in a GST refund when you file your GST return. Many times, taxpayers believe that there must be some kind of mistake! The government is paying them money! After all these years of paying the government GST when they file their tax returns, they're amazed.

But it is possible, and happens very frequently, that the government will pay the taxpayer instead of the other way around. And refunding the GST on capital purchases is one of the common reasons for this occurrence.

Tax Beater

Remember to include input tax credits on capital purchases used in your business.

GST on capital purchases is refundable as long as the capital item is being used for business purposes. So don't forget to include it as an input tax credit and get back the GST you deserve.

Can I Claim Input Tax Credits on Personal Capital Property?

You can generally claim a full input tax credit on personal capital property as long as you use the property in your business for at least 50% of the time and your business sales are subject to GST. Personal capital property refers to most types of capital assets like vehicles, computers, and office equipment. Personal capital property does not include real property like land and buildings and small capital purchases like software and small tools costing less than $200.

For example, if you purchased a computer which you use 75% of the time in your business and 25% of the time personally, you would still be eligible to claim an input tax credit of 100% of the GST paid (provided that your business was registered for GST and sold only taxable goods and services). If you purchased a vehicle costing less than $24,000, which is used 55% of the time for business purposes and 45% for personal purposes, you still would be eligible for the full input tax credit. On the other hand, if you purchased some furniture which is used 45% of the time for business purposes, and 55% of the time for personal purposes, you would not be eligible to claim any input tax credit for the GST you paid.

With real property like land and buildings, the property must be used exclusively (or at least 90% of the time) in your taxable business activities in order to qualify to claim any input tax credit. Therefore, most home-based entrepreneurs will not be able to claim an input tax credit on any GST they paid on the purchase of their home, as it will be nearly impossible to meet the 90% taxable business use criterion.

Tax Beater

Claim Input Tax Credits on personal capital property used more than 50% of the time in your taxable business.

Tax Beater

Claim Input Tax Credits on general operating expenses for items used more than 10% of the time in a taxable business.

Can I Claim Full Input Tax Credits on All General Business Expenses?

There are limitations to the amount of input tax credits you can claim on your business's operating expenses. General operating expenses are all the normal expenses that you incur on a day-to-day basis and might include office supplies, utilities, and repairs and maintenance.

If general operating expenses are used in your business 90% of the time or more and all of your business sales are subject to GST, then you will be able to claim 100% of the input tax credit on the GST you paid.

On the other hand, if the business use of an operating expense is 10% or less, then you will not be able to claim *any* input tax credit on the GST you paid. Anywhere in between and you will be able to claim only a portion of the input tax credit.

For example, assume that your business involves the developing of web sites for the Internet. You are registered for GST and all of your sales are taxable. Assume that you purchased some blank computer diskettes for your business. If you expect that the diskettes will be used 90% of the time or greater in your web site design business, then you would be able to deduct 100% of the GST on those diskettes.

On the other hand, if the diskettes might be used only 60% of the time for your business and the other 40% of the time they are used to store computer games and personal items, then you would be eligible to claim only 60% of the input tax credits.

If you purchase the diskettes and they are rarely used in the business, you would not be able to claim any input tax credit for the GST you paid on their purchase.

There is also a limitation on claiming input tax credits if you are engaged in another business activity that sells exempt goods and services. You must prorate the GST on a reasonable basis between the two businesses and then claim an input tax credit on the taxable business.

For example, assume that you have the web site design business but you also have a business selling life insurance. The selling of life insurance is an exempt business; therefore, purchases relating to that business would not qualify for an input tax credit. Say you purchased the computer diskettes for both the web site design business and the life insurance business and the allocation between the two businesses is 60% and 40% respectively. You would therefore be allowed to claim an input tax credit of 60% on the GST paid because 60% of the purchase related to the taxable web site design business.

Are There Any Other Restrictions on Claiming Input Tax Credits?

There are many restrictions on claiming input tax credits. This is one reason the legislation is so complex. Many of the restrictions would not involve the typical small-business entrepreneur. However, there are a few which would be common among many small-business owners.

The first such restriction relates to meals and entertainment expenses. For general income tax purposes you are eligible to claim only 50% of meals and entertainment expenses as a business deduction. New rules in Quebec have further reduced this restriction to 1% of gross revenue for general income tax purposes. The GST legislation mirrors the income tax legislation in this area by allowing you to claim an input tax credit of only 50% of the GST paid on meals and entertainment.

Another restriction relates to the GST paid on membership fees or dues paid to any recreational, dining, or sporting facility. For example, the GST paid on your golf membership, the fitness club membership, or your dues at the hunting and fishing club would not be eligible for an input tax credit. Even if there is a legitimate business reason for having the membership, the GST would not be eligible for the tax credit, just as the membership would not be deductible as a business expense under the *Income Tax Act*. The one exception might be if you purchase memberships and then resell them as part of your business.

If you purchase a passenger vehicle that costs more than $24,000, you will be restricted on how much of an input tax credit you can claim. Normally, if you use your vehicle more than 50% of the time for business purposes, you can claim 100% of the GST you paid on the purchase of the vehicle as an input tax credit. However, there is a restriction on the input tax credit you can claim on passenger vehicles that cost more than $24,000, even if the vehicle is used more than 50% in the business. With passenger vehicles, the maximum input tax credit you can claim is equal to 7% of $24,000, or $1,680. This restriction parallels the restriction in the *Income Tax Act* on deducting passenger vehicles in a business. This will be discussed more in Round 10.

When Do I Have to File My GST Return?

When you register for the GST, Revenue Canada will assign you a reporting period based on your anticipated level of sales. As your sales levels fluctuate, your reporting requirements may also fluctuate. If you have taxable sales of less than $6,000,000 annually, you will have an option of how you want to file your GST return. If your sales are greater than $6,000,000, there is no option, you must file your GST return monthly.

If your taxable sales are $500,000 or less, Revenue Canada will assign an annual reporting period for your business. This will mean that you will have to file your GST return only once a year. It will be due for filing three months after the year-end of your business. You do have the option, however, to change the reporting period to monthly or quarterly. There are times when this may be advantageous.

If you are in a business that is generating consistent GST refunds, you may want to consider electing to file your GST return on a quarterly or monthly basis. For example, if the majority of your sales are export sales or you are a farmer or fisherman with zero-rated taxable sales, then it is likely you will be generating GST refunds on a regular basis. If you file annually, you will get that refund only at the end of the year. If you move to a quarterly or monthly filing system, you will speed up the GST refunds. This will help the cash flow in your business.

The trade off with speeding up the GST refunds is, of course, having to file the GST returns more often. Although the forms are not that difficult to complete, whether the extra hassle is worth getting your money earlier is a personal judgement call.

Tax Beater

Speed up Input Tax Credit refunds by electing to file quarterly or monthly.

If, on the other hand, you always have to remit GST, then there is no real advantage to speeding up the process. Filing once a year will be the simplest approach and will provide the least administrative burden. If you normally have to pay GST, the government will usually request that you make four quarterly instalments to prepay the next year's GST liability. Therefore, annual filing only provides some administrative savings. Often from a cash flow point of view there is no savings, as you are required to remit GST instalments on a quarterly basis.

If your taxable sales for the year are greater than $500,000 but less than $6,000,000, you will be assigned a quarterly reporting period. When your sales are in this range, you will not have the option of filing annually. Your income is too great. On the other hand, you will have the option of filing monthly.

Tax Beater

Reduce hassles and reporting costs by filing GST returns only as required.

Once again, moving up to a monthly reporting period can make a lot of sense if your business is generating significant GST refunds. If your business is primarily selling to foreign countries or you are selling some other zero-rated product or service, then speeding up the GST refunds makes good business sense.

When Are the GST Returns Due?

If you are filing your GST return on an annual basis, the return is due, along with any remittance required, three months after the year-end of your business. If, as an annual filer, you are required to make quarterly instalments, the instalment is due one month after the end of your business quarter.

For example, if your business has a December year-end, the annual GST return will be due by March 31 and your first instalment will be due by April 30. If, on the other hand, you had a January year-end, the annual GST return would be due by April 30 and your first instalment would be due by May 31. April 30 would be the first quarter for your business year; therefore, your first instalment would be due one month after your first quarter, or May 31.

If you are required, or elect, to file your GST returns on a quarterly basis, you will be required to file your GST return, along with any remittance, if applicable, within one month after that quarterly reporting period. For example, if your year-end is December, your first quarterly reporting period will be from January 1 to March 31, and the return for the reporting period, along with any payment required, will be due by April 30.

If you are required, or elect, to file your GST returns on a monthly basis, you will be required to file your GST return, along with any remittance, if applicable, within one month after that monthly reporting period. So in this case, you will need to file the GST return for the month of January by the end of February and February's by the end of March and so on.

What Happens If I'm Late in Filing My GST Return?

If you owe GST to the government and you are late in remitting the GST, you will be charged a penalty and interest on the insufficient payment. Revenue Canada will charge you a penalty of 6% per year on any GST not remitted on time. In addition, the government will charge interest on the late remittance. Both the penalty and the interest are compounded daily and are not tax deductible. This is a significant penalty for not complying with the rules, especially when you consider that interest paid to the bank is normally tax deductible. This concept will be discussed in more detail in Round 7.

Tax Beater

Remit your GST on time.

This penalty and interest are also applicable to late payments of instalments. If you file your GST return on an annual basis, you may be required to make quarterly instalments. If you are late paying these instalments, you will be assessed the penalty and interest.

If you are owed a refund, no penalty or interest will accrue, since there is no liability. In fact, if Revenue Canada is slow in processing your refund, they will pay you interest beginning 21 days after you have filed your GST return for the current and any outstanding prior periods. It is still important to file your GST return on time, even if there is no activity. Filing your GST return on time, even if it is a "nil return" with no transactions, will ensure that future refunds are processed quickly and it will stop Revenue Canada from mailing out to you a request for a GST return.

What Happens If My Customer Doesn't Pay His Account?

When you make a sale and invoice your customer, you must remit the GST on the sale for that reporting period, regardless of when you collect the account. For example, assume that you have a December year-end and you are filing your GST returns on a quarterly basis. In February you made a sale to a customer for $1,000 and charged the customer $70 in GST. You delivered your product and the customer agreed to pay in 90 days.

Since you are filing your GST returns on a quarterly basis, you will have to remit the $70 of GST collected, net of any input tax credits, one month after the end of your first quarter, or by April 30. The $70 must be remitted, even though you haven't collected the money from your customer.

If your customer doesn't pay the account and you write the account off as a bad debt, make sure you remember to deduct the GST written off on the next GST return. To do this, deduct the amount of GST not collected on line 107 of the GST tax return. You have up to four years from the time you wrote off the bad debt to claim the GST. So you may want to review the accounts that you have written off over the past four years to ensure you claimed a refund of the GST.

Many provincial sales tax systems work the same way, requiring you to remit the provincial sales tax at the time a sale is made, not when the money is collected. Therefore, if you charged provincial sales tax on the sale, remember to apply for the refund of this tax as well. The time frame for going back and claiming a refund on old written-off accounts will vary from province to province. If you are considering reviewing your old files to claim a refund on an old bad debt, you should call your regional sales tax office to clarify the period within which your province will accept a late adjustment.

Tax Beater

Remember to request a refund of the GST and PST on accounts receivable that you have written off.

Do I Charge GST on the Sale of Used Capital Assets?

For whatever reason, selling used capital assets seems to cause more GST problems then any other area. It's likely because, with most businesses, a system is in place to capture the GST for all of the regular sales and purchases. But sales of old, used equipment don't happen every day. Thus, the GST is often forgotten.

As a GST registrant, you are required to charge GST on all sales in your business, which includes sales of used capital assets. Even though these sales are not typical for your business, you are still required to charge GST and remit the tax. So when you sell that old computer to your neighbour's child for $200, you have to charge $14 GST on the sale. If you don't, you will be liable for paying that GST if you're ever audited.

Tax Beater

Remember to charge GST on the sale of used capital assets or you will be paying the tax out of your pocket.

One of the most often forgotten areas for charging GST is on the trade-in of the business vehicle. When you trade your old truck in for a new truck, you are, in effect, selling to the dealership your old truck for the trade-in value. They, in turn, are selling you the new truck. You should inform the dealership that you are a GST registrant and that you will have to bill them for the GST. With most dealerships you can just provide them your GST registration number and they will enter this on the bill of sale in the area designated for the trade-in vehicle.

Tax Beater

Don't forget to charge and remit the GST on the trade-in of business vehicles or you will be liable for the GST.

Before the deal is done, when the dealership states what your old truck is worth on the trade-in, you might want to ask if that is including or excluding GST. If you think it is excluding GST, and the dealership thinks it is including, you might have a problem on your hands.

When the deal is done, remember that you are responsible for remitting the GST you collected on the sale or trade-in of your used truck. However, you are also eligible for an input tax credit on the GST you paid on the purchase of the new truck, provided the vehicle will be used primarily for business purposes.

ROUND SEVEN

365 Days to Save

$\mathbf{M}$any times a client will come into my office to discuss how to save taxes. The client will want to talk about complex corporate reorganizations or fancy uses of trusts. Once I sit down with them and discuss what's involved and the costs of these plans, they often lose interest.

Then I ask if they paid their taxes on time last year, as I advised. I ask how they purchased that new car. And the answers I get make me shake my head. Many people are looking for the knockout punch, that one great plan that will shelter all their money from tax. Yet they forget that saving tax dollars occurs throughout the year by doing a lot of little things correctly, little things like filing their tax returns on time or making tax instalments.

When Is My Tax Return Due?

This should be one of the simplest questions going. *Everyone* knows that your tax return is due April 30 each year, unless the government gives us an extension due to April 30 falling on a weekend. However, for self-employed individuals and their spouses, the tax return filing date became somewhat more complicated in 1995.

Starting in 1995, if you reported self-employment income on your tax return, you, and in most cases your spouse, could delay filing your tax returns until June 15. However, if any income taxes are owing on these returns, these taxes are due on April 30.

Tax Beater

File your tax return and pay any balance owing by April 30 to avoid being charged interest.

What this means is, unless you are really confident that you don't have a tax liability, you will have to complete your tax return by April 30 in order to calculate how much you owe to the government. And if you're going to complete your tax return to estimate your tax liability and pay your taxes by April 30, you might just as well file your return by April 30, too.

So it isn't much of a filing extension. Since interest will be charged on any insufficient payment, as a general rule, I do not recommend making use of the filing deadline extension and instead recommend that you keep filing your tax return by April 30.

Why Should I File My Tax Return on Time?

So few people realize that performing simple things like filing their tax returns when due can, over time, significantly increase a person's wealth. Consider two individuals, who both, every year, have to pay $6,000 when they file their tax returns in April. Taxpayer A files her tax return on time. Taxpayer B always procrastinates and doesn't get around to filing his tax return until September each year, after a nice relaxing summer. Say this goes on for 15 years, and over that 15-year period the average return on invested income is 8%. Taxpayer A will find herself in a much better position, in fact having as much as $38,000 more wealth, just by doing such a simple thing as filing her tax return on time. Why? Let me explain.

The government tries to discourage taxpayers from filing their tax returns late by charging interest and penalties. For every month or part month that your tax payment is late after April 30, you are charged interest at a rate set by the government. The rate is set quarterly and is based on the 90-day T-bill rate. For the calculation of the interest charged on late tax payments, the government adds an additional 4% to the base prescribed rate. For our example, we'll assume that the average interest rate to be charged over the 15 years will be 10%.

Since Taxpayer B doesn't file his tax return until September, he will be charged a penalty for late filing of 5% on the balance owing on the tax return, plus 1% for every month or part month that the tax return is late, to a maximum of 17%. For repeat offenders, the penalty is double, 10% plus 2% for each month or part month to a maximum of 20 months. The repeat offender penalty only kicks in if the taxpayer has been notified in writing to file a tax return.

In our example, this will mean that Taxpayer B will incur a penalty in the first year of 10% of the taxes outstanding, plus interest. In the second and subsequent years, the penalty will be 20%. Over the course of 15 years, Taxpayer B will pay approximately $21,500 in penalties and interest. If this money had been invested, instead of being paid to the government, it could have accumulated to $38,000 before taxes. This example has been exaggerated to prove a point. Remember, you can "Beat the Taxman" in many ways, but often the most effective ways are the easiest.

Tax Beater

Reduce the money you pay the government by paying and filing your tax return on time.

What Are Tax Instalments?

As a self-employed entrepreneur, you may be required to make income tax instalment payments. As your business becomes profitable, you will owe more tax. The government doesn't want to wait until the end of the year for you to pay that tax.

So instead, they request that you make instalments periodically throughout the year. Essentially, they are asking you to prepay your tax for the current year.

This is not uncommon. Employees do the same thing, only it is less painful. Their employer withholds a portion of their pay and remits it on their behalf to the government. The employee is effectively making tax instalments every time he or she gets paid. But they don't see the money, and since they don't have it to spend, making the instalment is not as difficult. They may not like it, but it is not as painful.

As a self-employed entrepreneur, making this tax instalment can be annoying. However, as you will see, the alternative is worse.

Do I Have to Make a Tax Instalment?

Whether or not you have to make a tax instalment depends on your tax situation in the previous two years. If your net tax owing, not including instalments, in either of the previous two years was greater than $2,000 (greater than $1,200 in Quebec), you will be required to make instalments in the next year.

If you are a resident of Quebec, your net tax owing is defined as your federal tax payable minus your federal tax deducted at source, your refundable Quebec abatement and your refundable credits.

If you are a resident anywhere else in Canada, your net tax owing is defined as your federal and provincial taxes payable minus your tax deducted at source and your refundable tax credits.

The net tax owing also includes any liability for the Canada Pension Plan (except Quebec residents).

When Are the Tax Instalments Due?

Tax instalments are due every March 15, June 15, September 15, and December 15 of the year. Farmers and fishermen have to make a tax instalment only on December 31.

If you are required to make instalments, Revenue Canada will mail you a reminder in February and August of each year.

Why Should I Make Tax Instalments?

Tax instalments appear to be a considerable hassle. So why should you make the instalments? Well, consider this. If you do not make your instalments on time or you do not remit sufficient instalments, Revenue Canada will assess you interest on the insufficient payment. This means that you will be borrowing from the government. And their interest rate is normally higher than what the bank would charge.

Not only is the interest rate charged by Revenue Canada higher than the bank rate, it is also not tax deductible. Had you borrowed from the bank to finance your business operations and thereby paid your tax instalments on time, you would have been eligible to deduct the interest expense and you would have saved tax dollars. However, interest paid to the government is not tax deductible. Using the government as a "bank" results in a significantly higher cost of borrowing!

AN EXAMPLE OF THE HIGH COST OF BORROWING FROM THE GOVERNMENT

Assumptions:
- Tax Liability of $10,000 outstanding for one year
- Average interest rate charged by the government is 10.5% (average rate for 1995)
- Average interest rate charged by the bank 8.65% (average bank prime for 1995)
- For the purposes of this example, interest is calculated on a simple interest basis

Alternative 1—Borrow from Government	$
Taxes outstanding for one year	10,000
Interest rate charged	10.5%
Interest paid and cost to the business	1,050

Alternative 2—Borrow from Bank

Bank loan outstanding for one year	10,000
Interest rate charged	8.65%
Interest paid	865
Tax deduction at 50% rate	(432)
Cost to the business	433
Savings from Borrowing from the Bank	**617**

Tax Beater

Pay your tax instalments as required to reduce your overall costs and increase profits.

And if this wasn't bad enough, Revenue Canada will assess a penalty if the instalment interest charges exceed $1,000 in a year. And of course, this penalty is not tax deductible either. When these interest charges and penalties are added together, not making instalments can be a very costly way to finance your business.

AN EXAMPLE OF HOW THE INSTALMENT PENALTY WORKS

Assumptions:
- Instalment interest charged $3,000
- No instalments paid during the year

	$
Penalty equals 50% of	
a) Instalment interest charged	3,000
Minus the greater of:	
b) $1,000 and	(1,000)
c) 25% of the instalment interest you would have paid if you had made no instalments during the year (25% of $3,000 or $750)	
	2,000
	50%
Instalment Penalty	**1,000**

What Are My Instalment Options?

You have three options to choose from in any one year to calculate the amount of your instalments. In some years, this can be very important to minimizing the amount of money you pay to the government and maximizing your cash flow. Remember, effective tax planning is deferring as long as possible the money you pay to the government. Making proper use of your instalment options is key to effective tax planning.

No-Calculation Option

Your first option, which is also the option that is automatically used by the government, is the "Second Preceding Year Option" or as Revenue Canada calls it, the "No-Calculation Option." If you are required to make tax instalments, Revenue Canada will notify you with reminder notices in February and August of each year. These reminder notices will indicate the amount of the tax instalment that you need to make to avoid any instalment interest charge. Revenue Canada uses the no-calculation option to calculate the instalments required on these reminder notices. This method of calculating the instalments is as follows:

- The March 15 and June 15 instalment is based on your second preceding taxation year. For example, your March 15 and June 15, 1997, tax instalments will be based on one-quarter of your net tax owing and any Canada Pension Plan (CPP) or Quebec Pension Plan (QPP) for the *second preceding tax year*, or in this case 1995.

- The September 15 and December 15 instalment is meant to be a catch-up payment. The idea is that by December 15 you will have paid to the government in instalments the amount of your net tax liability *of the previous year*. With that in mind, the government calculates your remaining two instalments by first deducting your March 15 and June 15 instalments from *your prior year's net tax liability*. This balance is then divided by two to arrive at your last two instalment payments.

AN EXAMPLE OF HOW THE "SECOND PRECEDING YEAR INSTALMENT OPTION" WORKS

Assumptions:

- Net tax owing for 1994 was $3,000
- Net tax owing for 1995 was $5,000

Question:

What are my required tax instalments for 1996 under the "Second Preceding Year Option"?

Date of Instalment	Calculation of Instalment	$
March 15, 1996	$3,000 ÷ 4	750
June 15, 1996	$3,000 ÷ 4	750
September 15, 1996	$5,000 – $750 – $750	
	= $3,500 ÷ 2	1,750
December 15, 1996	$5,000 – $750 – $750	
	= $3,500 ÷ 2	1,750
Total Instalments Paid		**5,000**

Tax Beater

Follow the "No-Calculation Option" when your income is stable or rising to minimize the amount of pre-paid tax.

Admittedly, this process is complicated, especially for something that should be as simple as making instalments. However, the system used prior to this one required you to make a March 15 instalment based on the net tax liability of the previous year which was due for filing on April 30—after the instalment was due. You were being asked to make an instalment before you were required to file your tax return which was used to calculate the instalment. And if you miscalculated the payment, you were charged interest!

The calculation of this instalment option is by far the most complicated. However, the nice thing is that you really don't need to understand how it is calculated. The more important thing to remember is this rule: If your income is stable or rising, you're better off using the "Second Preceding Year Option." Otherwise, consider one of the other two instalment options.

Prior-Year Option

The second instalment option is often referred to as the "Prior-Year Option." With this option you make instalments based on one-quarter of your prior year net tax owing. For example, if you are calculating your 1997 instalment contributions, then you would take your 1996 net tax owing, plus any CPP contributions payable, and divide this by four. This will provide you with four equal instalment payments for the year.

This instalment option can be very useful in years where your income is decreasing. For example, assume that Jane had a net tax liability in 1995 of $20,000. It was an excellent year, in which she won several major contracts. However, in 1996 she didn't have such a great year, which resulted in a net tax liability of only $6,000.

Tax Beater

Increase cash flow by electing to use alternative instalment options.

If she followed the second preceding year option as calculated by the government, she would make instalments of $5,000 on both March 15 and June 15 and then no instalments in September or December. Under the prior-year option, Jane could have made instalments of $1,500 on each of the four instalment dates, March 15, June 15, September 15, and December 15. By electing to use the prior-year option, Jane would have paid $4,000 less to the government and would have delayed paying the instalments longer.

Current-Year Option

The third and last instalment option is referred to as the "Current-Year Option." This option is similar to the prior-year method

Tax Beater

Use the "Current-Year Instalment Option" in years of declining income to maximize cash flow and personal wealth.

in that the instalments are equal throughout the year. However, instead of basing the instalments on the net tax liability of the prior year, the instalments are based on your estimate of your current year net tax liability.

This instalment option is extremely useful in years where you have a drop in income. For example, assume Jane had that really exceptional year in 1996 and had a net tax liability of $20,000. However, 1997 isn't shaping up to be a repeat year. Instead, she estimates that her net tax liability will be around $6,000.

If Jane used the prior-year instalment method, she would pay $5,000 on each of the four instalment dates. She would pay $20,000 over the course of the year, representing a significant cash drain on her business in a year that she is not doing as well.

Instead, if Jane estimates her next year properly and elects to use the current-year method, she could reduce her instalments from $20,000 for the year to $6,000 without being charged instalment interest. This is a significant improvement in cash flow, which, over time, will help to increase Jane's personal wealth.

A word of caution if you elect to use either the prior-year or current-year instalment options: If you incorrectly calculate your instalments or estimate your current year's tax liability incorrectly, and you do not remit enough in instalments during the year, Revenue Canada will charge you late instalment interest and possibly penalties. To assist you in calculating your proper instalments, you should consider using Revenue Canada's form T1033-WS, "Worksheet for Calculating 1997 Instalment Payments." It will greatly assist you in deciding which option is best for you.

What If I Miss a Tax Instalment?

Missing a tax instalment payment is just like borrowing money at a very high interest rate. This can be very costly to your business. So your objective should always be to make timely tax instalments. However, say, due to cash flow problems, procrastination, or simple forgetfulness, you missed one or two instalments. You can still reduce or eliminate any non-deductible interest charged by Revenue Canada by prepaying your next instalment.

For example, say you miss your March 15th instalment. You can eliminate most or all of the instalment interest charge by paying to the government an amount equal to the total of the March 15th, June 15th, and September 15th instalments on June 15th. By prepaying your September 15th instalment, Revenue Canada will offset the interest you earned on the prepayment against the interest you were charged on the late March 15th instalment.

Note, however, that prepaying your instalments will not earn you interest income. If you prepay your instalment, Revenue Canada will not pay you interest income, they will only reduce any instalment interest they were going to charge you for the year. Therefore, in the above example, if the September 15 instalment is substantially greater than the March 15 instalment, it isn't worth it to prepay the entire September instalment. Instead, only prepay an amount equal to the March instalment you missed.

Tax Beater

If you miss an instalment payment, catch up your instalments and prepay the next instalment to reduce or eliminate the non-deductible instalment interest charge.

What Is the Penalty for Forgetting to Remit Employee Deductions on Time?

If you have employees in your business or hire a family member to help you, remitting tax withholdings, CPP/QPP, and EI (Employment Insurance) payments on time is an integral part of reducing every day the money you pay to the government. By neglecting to remit these taxes on time, you increase the amount of money you pay to the government through increased interest and penalty payments.

Tax Beater

Properly withhold and remit payroll taxes on time.

Failure to withhold and remit tax, CPP/QPP, and EI for your employees results in a 10% penalty of the amount not remitted for each occurrence. For the second occurrence in the same year, the penalty can increase to 20% of the amount not remitted, if the failure to remit was made knowingly, intentionally, or due to gross negligence. And of course, these penalties will not be tax deductible.

When Are Employee Remittances Due for Filing?

If your average monthly payroll remittances for your second preceding calendar year were less than $15,000 per month, you must make your remittances by the 15th of the month following the month in which your payroll is paid. For example, if the current year is 1997, to determine your filing due date, you would look at what your average monthly payroll remittances were for the calendar year 1995. If the average monthly remittances were less than $15,000 per month, your due date for payroll remittances is the 15th of the month following the month your employees were paid.

If your average monthly payroll remittances for the second preceding calendar year were greater than $15,000 per month, the payroll remittances are more frequent. Most small business and home-based entrepreneurs are not likely to have this large a payroll. However, if you do fall into this category, see the table opposite for the frequency of the remittances.

If your payroll has been dropping such that you have gone below the $15,000 per month threshold, you can elect to make remittances based on the level of average monthly payroll remittances of the prior year, instead of the second preceding year. For example, if in 1995 your average monthly payroll remittances were $16,000, and in 1996 your average payroll remittances were $13,000, normally you would still be required to make payroll remittances twice a month. Under normal

Average Monthly Remittance for Second Preceding Year	Frequency and Timing of Remittance
Less than $15,000/month	15th day of the month following month in which payroll paid
Greater than $15,000/month and less than $50,000/month	1. Payroll paid before 16th day of the month, remittance due on or before 25th day of the month. 2. Payroll paid after 15th day of the month, remittance due on or before the 10th day of the following month.
Equal to or greater than $50,000/month	Remittance due by third day (not including Saturday, Sunday or holiday) after the end of the following periods in which the payments were made: 1. Period beginning on the 1st day and ending on the 7th day of the month. 2. Period beginning on the 8th day and ending on the 14th day of the month. 3. Period beginning on the 15th day ending on the 21st day of the month; and 4. Period beginning on the 22nd day and ending on the last day of the month.

circumstances you must look back to 1995 to determine your frequency of remittances for 1997.

However, you can elect to reduce your remittance frequency to once a month by advising Revenue Canada that you are electing to base your 1997 remittances on your 1996 average monthly payroll remittances. This should provide greater cash flow and fewer administrative hassles.

Tax Beater

Increase cash flow and save time by electing to reduce your payroll remittance frequency.

What Fines and Penalties Are Tax Deductible?

As discussed previously, interest and penalties paid to the government for late filing of your tax return or insufficient tax instalments are not tax deductible. However, there are some fines and penalties that you can deduct in your business. You are not, of course, going to go out looking to get fined, but if you do, knowing what is tax deductible can reduce the sting of the infraction.

The most common fine people usually ask about is speeding tickets. Speeding tickets are not tax deductible. Nor are most fines or penalties payable as a result of breaking the law. However there are some exceptions.

In deciding whether or not a fine or penalty is tax deductible, Revenue Canada looks at two criteria:

1. The fine or penalty must have been incurred as a normal risk of carrying on business, even though reasonable care was taken in avoiding it, and the imposition was beyond the control of the taxpayer and the taxpayer's employees.
2. The breach of the law causing the fine or penalty did not arise from negligence, ignorance, or disobedience of the law, nor did it endanger public safety.

Speeding tickets are a clear disobedience of the law, despite the fact that you may have been late for a client meeting. Accordingly, they are not tax deductible. An example often used as a possible deductible fine is overweight fines imposed on truckers. It may be argued that hauling an overweight trailer is a normal risk of carrying on business in the trucking industry and that reasonable care was taken to avoid the fine.

Also, it may be possible to deduct some fines imposed by trade associations that relate to your business. Another possible deduction is fines imposed for failure to meet a private contract, like not delivering your product or service on time. I have also argued under certain circumstances that parking tickets can be deductible. If the ticket was issued while you were on business, and you made an attempt to estimate your time and placed money in the meter accordingly, the ticket should be tax deductible if you were delayed and went overtime at the meter.

Interest and penalties paid to the government relating to your personal and corporate income tax are not deductible. However, *interest* paid on late or deficient payments of GST, sales tax, or excise tax that relate to a business will be deductible. *Penalties* imposed under the GST, sales tax, or excise tax legislation will not, however, be deductible.

It is also interesting to note that penalties imposed on default in payment of property and business taxes levied by a municipality are deductible if the taxes themselves are normally deductible in your business.

It certainly isn't wise to operate your business in a manner that is subjecting you to fines on a regular basis. However, if you are *fined,* knowing if you can deduct the fine for tax purposes will help to save you some money. If you're not sure if the fine you have been assessed is tax deductible, consult with your professional advisor or contact your local Revenue Canada district taxation office.

Tax Beater

Reduce the sting of infractions by knowing which fines and penalties are tax deductible.

How Can I Maximize My Deductible Interest?

For interest paid on borrowed money to be tax deductible, the loan must be for business reasons. It is not sufficient to say that 100% of your mortgage interest is tax deductible because you had enough savings to pay off the mortgage and then borrowed for your business. In order to make that interest tax deductible, you need to actually pay off your mortgage and then borrow for your business.

This is an area that Revenue Canada does watch quite closely. Many court cases have dealt with the issue of interest deductibility. And it is very clear that for a loan

Tax Beater

Turn personal loans into business loans and deduct the interest for tax purposes.

Tax Beater

Pay down personal loans before business loans to maximize your tax-deductible interest expense.

to be deductible, the loan *must* have been taken out for business purposes.

So, how can you maximize your deductible interest? Well, one way is exactly how I described above. If you have savings that you were going to use in your business and you have a mortgage or a personal car loan still outstanding, consider using your savings to pay off those loans. Then borrow what you need for the business, and use the house or car as security to obtain a lower interest rate. You will be in the same position as before, except now the interest will be tax deductible.

Consider also the situation where you have two loans. One is a business loan, where the interest is tax deductible. The other is a personal loan where the interest is not tax deductible. In most cases it will make more sense to pay off the personal loan first, before reducing the business loan. This will allow you to maximize your tax deductible interest expense.

Can I Deduct the Cost of Life Insurance?

Generally speaking, as a small-business entrepreneur, you cannot deduct the cost of life insurance. However, you may be able to arrange your affairs in such a way to make your life insurance premiums deductible.

Tax Beater

Structure business loans to turn non-deductible insurance premiums into tax-deductible expenditures.

In order for life insurance premiums to be tax deductible, the life insurance policy must be used as security for a business loan. In addition, the lender must require that the policy be used as security, the lending institution must be a Canadian bank, trust company, credit union, insurance company, or corporation whose principal business is lending money to strangers, *and* the interest on the loan must be normally tax deductible.

By structuring your bank borrowings to take advantage of these restrictions, it may be possible to turn a non-deductible expense into a tax deductible expenditure.

How Can I Maximize the Tax Savings on the Courses I Take?

It is surprising, but a simple thing like taking a course relating to your business can become very complex when you're determining how the course fees are treated for tax purposes. There are four alternative income tax treatments when it comes to course fees. Knowing these rules may assist you in deciding which course to take, if you have to choose among several.

The general rule relating to courses is that if the course is intended to maintain, update, or upgrade an existing skill that relates to your business, the costs associated with the course would be fully deductible. This means that if you are at the highest tax level, the course would be deductible at that rate, or approximately 50%.

If the course is taken to learn a new skill, the costs of the course are not fully deductible, but are instead treated as a capital expense. If the course relates to your business, you would be able to deduct over time a portion of the course as an eligible capital expenditure. (Eligible capital expenditure is discussed in more detail in Round 9.)

If the course did not relate to your business at all, the expenses would not be tax deductible, regardless of whether the course is developing a new skill or updating an existing skill.

The last possible tax treatment would be to claim the course as a tax credit on your personal tax return. If the course qualifies for a tuition tax credit, then Revenue Canada takes the view that it must be claimed that way, despite the fact that the course may have been taken to upgrade an existing skill and be deductible as a business expense. By claiming the course as a tuition tax credit, you are eligible for tax savings of only approximately 27%. If the course was deductible in your business, then you could have received a tax savings of up to 53%.

Tax Beater

Maximize your tax savings on course fees by taking those courses that are fully deductible for income tax purposes.

In summary, if the course is eligible for the tuition tax credit, Revenue Canada says you must claim it as a credit. If it is not
eligible for the tuition tax credit and it relates to your business,
then the costs can either be fully deducted as a business expense
or deducted over time as an eligible capital expenditure,
depending on whether the course is developing a new skill or
not. If the course does not at all relate to your business and it is
not eligible for the tuition tax credit, then it will not be tax
deductible.

How Can I Maximize My Tax Savings on the Conventions I Attend?

Attending conventions is an excellent way to meet people with
similar business interests, review the newest products, develop
new customer contacts, and refresh your skills in your discipline. But if you're going to spend the money to attend a convention, you want to make sure that it will be tax deductible.

With tax savings in mind, there are a couple of things you
should be aware of relating to conventions. First, you are
allowed to deduct the costs of attending only *two* conventions a
year. You should keep this in mind as you plan which conventions you want to attend.

Second, in order to deduct the costs of the convention, the
convention must be for business purposes. This rules out your
Star Trek convention, unless your business is selling Star Trek
products!

Tax Beater

Know which
conventions are
tax deductible and
attend accordingly.

Third, the convention must be held in an area that
covers the geographical area of the organizer of the convention. This is meant to discourage a Canadian company from organizing a winter convention for Canadian
business people in Florida. However, it would be perfectly acceptable for you to attend a convention in Florida that was sponsored by a Florida company and related
to your business interests in Canada.

You can save tax dollars by knowing which conventions will be allowed as a tax deduction before attending the convention. These decisions have to be made throughout the year, not in April when you're filing your tax return.

Why Is Some of My Business Advertising Not Tax Deductible and How Can I Ensure 100% Will Be Deductible?

Despite the fact that you may advertise your product or service to a Canadian audience in a newspaper or magazine distributed in Canada, you may find that the advertising is not tax deductible. This can occur if one of the following (or other) restrictions apply: the newspaper or magazine you advertise in is not owned by Canadians; it is not edited by Canadian residents; it is not printed in Canada or the United States.

The idea here is that the government wants to encourage Canadians to buy Canadian. When we advertise to the Canadian public, the government wants us to use Canadian print media. They don't want us to use foreign magazines to market primarily in Canada.

This relates also to television and radio advertising. Advertising expenses paid to U.S. radio and television stations that are primarily directed to the Canadian audience will not be deductible for tax purposes.

To ensure your advertising dollars are deductible, ask a few questions like: Who owns the paper or magazine? Where is the material printed? Where is the editing done? If you're not getting satisfactory answers or you're still not sure, contact your local Revenue Canada taxation office. They should be able to tell you if your advertising dollars will be tax deductible.

Tax Beater

When advertising to the Canadian public, advertise with Canadian media to ensure your advertising dollars are tax deductible.

What Are Some Year-End Tax-Saving Tips?

As I said at the beginning of the Round, saving tax dollars occurs 365 days a year. And one of those key days is the day you complete your tax return. The following are a couple of tax-saving tips to consider when you're filling out that T1 General form.

- **Value your inventory**: Consider writing off obsolete or damaged inventory, thereby reducing your taxes. If you sell products, and provided you are not using the cash method of accounting (see Round 2), then you must add up the value of your inventory at the year-end of your business. The value of your year-end inventory, or ending inventory, is not an expense to your business. It will *become* an expense when the product is sold.

Tax Beater

Reduce taxes by not including in your year-end inventory, obsolete, or damaged goods.

If you include in ending inventory obsolete and/or damaged goods, then you are deferring the tax deduction of those expenses. Instead, never include in ending inventory, obsolete, or damaged goods in order to maximize tax savings.

- **Allow for your slow payers:** If you have clients who are slow in paying the money they owe you, allow for them. Provided you are not using the cash method of accounting, you will be required to include in your income the amounts your customers owe you, despite the fact that they have not paid you yet.

Tax Beater

Provide for doubtful paying customers and defer tax dollars.

If you consider it doubtful that a particular customer will, in fact, pay you, why pay taxes on that revenue? Instead, allow for the receivable by not including it in your outstanding accounts receivable balance. This does not mean that you have given up collecting on the receivable. If the customer pays later, just include the amount paid in that year's income.

- **Waive your penalties and interest charges:** If you have been charged a penalty or interest, consider requesting to have the penalty and interest charges reversed. Revenue Canada will, on occasion, reverse these charges. However, you must provide them with an exceptional reason why you were unable to comply with the law, resulting in the assessing of penalties and interest.

Revenue Canada has cited the following examples of circumstances which may be acceptable in reversing penalties and interest, if these circumstances prevented a taxpayer from complying with the law:

1. natural or human-made disasters such as a flood or a fire
2. civil disturbances or disruptions in services such as a postal strike
3. a serious illness or accident
4. serious emotional or mental distress such as a death in the immediate family.

As well, penalties and interest may be waived if Revenue Canada delayed in informing you of an amount owing, or if you were relying on material made available to the public and the material contained incorrect information.

If you receive incorrect advice from Revenue Canada, you shouldn't be charged interest or penalties. If Revenue Canada tells you that you don't have to make instalments and then later charges you late instalment interest, you should be able to get that interest reversed.

In addition, if Revenue Canada makes an error in processing, interest and penalties should not be charged on the error. Or if Revenue Canada delays in providing the necessary information to make the appropriate instalment or payments, you may be able to get the interest and penalty reversed.

Tax Beater

Consider requesting Revenue Canada to reverse interest and penalties.

One other situation where it may be possible to waive interest and penalties is in severe hardship cases. If you are having severe difficulty in paying your outstanding taxes, the government may waive the interest and penalties in order to recover the outstanding tax liability.

In summary, don't just give up if you have been assessed interest and penalties. In the right circumstances, you may be able to get them reversed.

ROUND EIGHT

Home Sweet Home

Operating your home-based business as a sole proprietor can provide many tax benefits. Deducting a portion of your home expenses is a goal for every home-based entrepreneur. In this Round we will look at the rules for deducting these home expenses.

Am I Eligible to Deduct Home Expenses?

The most publicized tax savings for home-based businesses is the deduction of home expenses. This is so attractive because it allows you to deduct costs that would normally not be tax deductible. In order to be eligible to deduct home expenses from your home-based business, you must meet one of the following criteria:

- your home must be your principal place of business; or

- you use a designated area in your home for the sole

purpose of earning your business income, and you use this space on a regular and ongoing basis to meet clients.

For most home-based businesses, meeting these criteria is not a problem. However, for some businesses that have an office located outside the home, meeting these criteria may be more difficult. Where your home is not your principal place of business, ensure that you designate an area in your home to be used solely for your business. This means that the family room should not be used as your office, unless you're willing to kick everyone else out of that room. In addition, you must be prepared to meet clients in your office and be able to demonstrate to Revenue Canada that you in fact do meet clients at home. By taking these extra steps, you can ensure that you can deduct home expenses in your business.

In most cases, however, the home-based entrepreneur's principal place of business will be the home. In this case, it is not necessary to conduct client meetings at home. However, in order to maximize the deduction of home expenses, you should still designate an area in your home to be used solely for business purposes. By doing so, you will maximize the deduction of home expenses. If you cannot designate an area to be used solely in your business, fear not, you can still deduct home expenses, just not as much.

How Do I Calculate The Home Expense Deductions?

If your principal place of business is at home, you can deduct a reasonable percentage of home expenses. How much you can deduct is usually determined by the following formula: divide the business area in your home by the overall square footage of your home, and multiply by the eligible

Tax Beater

If your home is not your principal place of business, designate an area in your home to be used solely for business purposes and conduct client meetings at home.

Tax Beater

If your home is your principal place of business, maximize your tax deductions by designating an area in your home to be used exclusively for your business.

expenses. For example, assume that you have converted the spare bedroom to be used solely in your business. If your spare bedroom has a floor space of 120 square feet and the total area of your home is 1,200 square feet, the amount of eligible home expenses that can be deducted is 120 divided by 1,200, or 10% of the eligible expenses.

If you cannot designate an area in your home for your business, you will have to pro-rate the approximate time the area is used for business purposes as compared to personal use. For example, assume you use the family room during the day while everyone else is either at work or school, and at night the room is once again used by the family. Say it works out that you use the room 60% of the time for business purposes. Assuming that the room represents 25% of the square footage of the house, you would be able to deduct 60% of 25%, or 15% of eligible home expenses.

You may be able to increase the business use of your home by including the hallway to your home office and front foyer. If you are meeting clients in your home, you will likely hang your clients coat up in the front foyer, your client will have to make use of the hallway to get to your office and to leave at the end of the meeting. In this case, more than just your office is being used for business purposes. Note that unless clients use a separate entrance to your home, you will have to estimate the amount of time the hallway and foyer are being used for business purposes in comparison to personal use.

As can be seen from the way tax deductible home expenses are calculated, you can obtain tax savings by maximizing the area used in your business or reducing the area in your home. You can increase the area used in your business by making use of a larger room in your home for your business. A way to reduce the area of your home is to exclude, for example, your basement, if it is not usable living space.

Tax Beater

Maximize the home area used in your business or minimize the area of your home.

What Kind of Home Expenses Can I Deduct?

Eligible home expenses include interest on your mortgage, house insurance, heat, electricity, water, maintenance and repairs to your home, property taxes, and any other general house expenses. A portion of any of these expenses can be deducted from your business income. In Quebec, these expenses are restricted by a further 50% due to changes in that province's 1996 budget.

Tax Beater

New or increased home costs that are a direct result of your business can be deducted 100% as a business expense.

Any expenses that relate directly to your business can be deducted 100% in your business. For example, if you have an increase in your insurance premium due to your business operations, you should deduct 100% of this increase.

Telephone and other consumable supplies are not considered home expenses and are therefore not subject to the area reduction. You can deduct a reasonable amount of these costs that relate to your business. For example, you can deduct a reasonable allocation of the line charge based on usage. Long distance charges that relate specifically to your business are tax deductible. If your business requires considerable use of the phone, you should consider having a separate telephone line for your business. This way, 100% of the phone costs will be tax deductible.

Tax Beater

A separate telephone line for your business is 100% tax deductible.

Are There Any Limitations on Deducting Home Expenses?

In the start-up years of many businesses, it is common not to make a profit. It often takes some time to establish your client base, to perfect your offering and generate sufficient sales to cover your costs. The low overhead you achieve by working at home helps, but is not always enough. It is important to realize that in deducting home expenses, you cannot create a loss or increase a loss through the deduction of home expenses.

For example, assume that after recording your direct business income and expenses (excluding home expenses) you have a net profit of $100. If the business portion of home expenses is $150, you would only be able to deduct $100 in the current year, bringing your net income to $0. The balance of $50 can be carried forward for as long as you are in business.

If your direct business income and expenses resulted in a net loss of $100 before deducting home expenses, you would not be able to deduct *any* home expenses, because you cannot increase the loss of $100 by deducting home expenses. However, these home expenses can be carried forward to be deducted in a future year where your business is profitable.

These rules provide some very important tax-saving ideas. First of all, even if your business is losing money and you cannot deduct the home expenses in the current year, you must keep track of those home expenses so that they can be deducted in a future year. Revenue Canada is not going to deduct these expenses for you. It is up to you to record the information and deduct these expenses in a profitable year.

Tax Beater

Keep track of the business portion of home expenses so each year you can deduct them either in the current year or in a profitable year.

Another very important tax-saving technique that arises from these restrictions is to properly classify home expenses. With many expenses the distinction is clear. For example, property taxes relate to your home overall; therefore, the business portion is subject to the above restrictions. However, with other expenses the distinction may not be so clear-cut. For example, if you purchase a separate insurance rider for your business, you can deduct this cost, regardless of the above restriction, because it is a business expense. Or, if you increase your mortgage to help finance the start-up of your business, that portion of the mortgage interest that relates to the business is a business expense which you can deduct regardless of whether or not your business is profitable.

Tax Beater

Maximize your tax savings by properly classifying the business portion of home expenses from business expenses.

This distinction between expenses that are subject to the profitability test and those that are not is important, especially where you have other sources of income. If you are receiving a pension or have other sources of income, the maximizing of your business loss will significantly reduce the amount of tax you pay.

Capital vs. Expense: A Wealth of Distinction

One of the most important distinctions in tax, one that can result in significant tax savings if you get it right, is the distinction between a capital item and an expense item. If you make a mistake in this area and treat something as a capital expenditure instead of as an expense, you may find it will take five, ten, twenty years to fully deduct the cost of that purchase. Alternatively, being too aggressive and deducting capital expenditures as an expense could open you up to scrutiny from Revenue Canada and reassessment. Finding that balance between capital and expense can be difficult, but the rewards are that you win Round 9 and definitely "Beat the Taxman."

What Is a Capital Expenditure?

Determining if a purchase should be capitalized or expensed will depend on many factors. With some purchases, it is clear-cut. There is very little room for maneuvering. For example, when you purchase a building or a car, these are obviously capital purchases. However, what about replacing the roof on the house or placing a new engine in the car? Are these capital or expense purchases? There is no definitive answer to this question. Each situation must be reviewed on a case-by-case basis. In order to assist you in making the capital/expense distinction, I have laid out some of the general rules Revenue Canada uses and examples for you to follow.

The first rule is whether or not the expenditure provides a lasting benefit—that is, can this item reasonably be expected to last a few years or more. If so, the expenditure will normally be considered a capital purchase. For example, the purchase of a computer provides a benefit to the business over a number of years and therefore should be a capital expenditure. The legal fees paid to incorporate a company will benefit the company for many years and, therefore, are considered a capital expenditure. Course fees paid to learn a new skill will benefit you for many years as you practise that skill, so they too are considered a capital expenditure.

The second rule is whether the expenditure is considered maintenance or an improvement. If the expenditure is merely restoring the property to its original condition, it would be considered an expense. For example, replacing a roof to bring the building back to its original condition is an expense. Replacing an old roof with a new, better quality, more durable roof would be seen as an improvement and be treated as a capital expenditure.

A third rule is whether the expenditure is considered to be for repair to an integral part of an existing asset or for a separate asset altogether. For example, the replacement of tires on a company vehicle would be considered an expense item, because even though the tires are themselves a separate asset, they form an integral part of the company vehicle. On the other hand, the cost of replacing a lathe in your workshop would be regarded as a capital expenditure because the lathe is not an integral part of the workshop.

The fourth rule concerns the relative value of the expenditure in comparison to the value of the whole property or to other repair and maintenance costs. The purchase of a spark plug for an engine is a separate asset, but no one would consider it anything other than an expense to maintain the engine. On the other hand, the purchase of an entirely new engine may be considered capital, given the significant cost of such a repair to the vehicle.

The fifth rule concerns repairs or installation costs for new and used property. If you purchase used equipment that requires repairs to make it suitable for use, then the repairs would be considered capital, even if the repairs would normally have been considered an expense. This is because the repairs are really considered a part of the purchase of the equipment. Similarly, the cost of installing equipment will be considered a part of the purchase of the equipment. For example, if you have to hire an electrician to hook up a new table saw, the cost of the hook-up would be considered part of the cost of the equipment.

The sixth and last rule concerns repairs made in anticipation of or as a condition of the sale of the property. Where this is the case, the repairs are normally considered a capital expenditure. On the other hand, if the repairs were going to be made in any event, and did not relate to the anticipated sale, the repairs would remain as an expense.

Once you have decided that an expenditure is capital, you must then decide how and if it can be deducted. There are three categories to consider. The first category is *non-deductible expenditures*. Land is a good example of this category, or assets you have purchased for your personal use only. You cannot deduct the cost of land or personal use items.

Tax Beater

Maximize tax savings by knowing the difference between a capital and an expense purchase.

The second category is *depreciable property*. This is the most common category for capital purchases and would include computers, automobiles, and most other tangible assets that you would buy for your business.

The third category is *eligible capital expenditures*. These include the non-tangible assets like the incorporation costs. This category will be discussed in more detail in this Round.

Included in the Appendix is a list of some of the more common capital expenditures for small and home-based businesses.

What Is Capital Cost Allowance (CCA)?

A common capital expenditure for small-business entrepreneurs is the purchase of depreciable property. Depreciable property purchased for business purposes can be deducted on your tax return, but not all at once. Instead of being able to deduct depreciable property immediately as an expense, you can only deduct these expenditures over time in the form of depreciation. Revenue Canada calls this *depreciation capital cost allowance* or CCA.

To ensure that everyone depreciates similar assets at the same rate, the government has set the rates for depreciating certain assets. This is done by setting up different classes of assets. For example, the computer you purchased would be included in class 10 and can be depreciated at a rate of 30% per year. That bookcase would be a class 8 asset and can be depreciated at a rate of 20% per year. By establishing these classes and what assets go into each class, the government can ensure that no one gets an unfair advantage by depreciating assets too quickly and deferring tax. I have included in the Appendix a list of common asset purchases made by small and home-based businesses, their classes, and the rate of depreciation or CCA you can claim.

Are There Any Special Rules in the Year of Purchase?

Most capital assets that are purchased are eligible for only half the maximum capital cost allowance in the year of purchase. For example, if you purchased a computer for $3,000, the computer would qualify as a class 10 asset, which would mean that it can be depreciated at a maximum rate of 30% per year. However, in the year you purchased the computer you can claim only half of the normal CCA on the new computer purchase. The next year, you will be able to claim the full 30% on the remaining balance.

Tax Beater

Claim full depreciation on assets not subject to the half-rate rule.

It's important to note, though, that not all assets you purchase are subject to this half-rate rule. There are a handful of purchases that are exempt from this rule. The list of common asset purchases for small and home-based businesses included in the Appendix notes which assets are not subject to the half-rate rule. You can score a few points by ensuring you claim full CCA on these assets.

What Happens When I Sell an Asset?

When you sell a capital asset, you have to reduce the balance of the class to which the capital asset relates by the lesser of the original cost of the asset or the proceeds you received on the sale. For example, assume you sell that computer you purchased for $3,000 to someone else for $2,000. We would reduce the value of class 10 by the lesser of the purchase price, $3,000, or the proceeds we received, $2,000.

If there is a balance remaining in the class and there are other assets that belong to that class that you still own, the balance is just carried forward for future CCA claims.

If there is a positive balance remaining in the class and there are no other assets belonging to that class that you still own, you can deduct the remaining balance in the current year. This is referred to as *claiming a terminal loss*. For example, assume the only asset in class 10 is the computer we bought for $3,000. In the first year we claimed CCA of $3,000 x 30% x ½ or $450. The 30% represents the maximum CCA rate for computer equipment and the ½ represents the half-rate rule. The balance remaining in the class would be $2,550 or $3,000 minus the $450 CCA. If we then sold the computer for $2,000, the balance remaining would be $550. If there were no other assets in class 10, the full $550 could be deducted in the current year to reduce income taxes.

Tax Beater

Claim terminal losses to maximize your tax savings.

If there is a negative balance remaining in the class, the negative balance must be added to income, regardless of whether or not there are any assets remaining in the class. This is referred to as *recapture*. For example, assume that instead of selling the computer in year two for $2,000, you sold it for $3,000. The balance in that class after the first year's CCA was $2,550. If you subtract $3,000 from that, you end up with a negative balance of $450. This must be added to your income in the current year.

Do I Have to Claim Full CCA?

Nowhere in the rules does it say that each year you have to claim full CCA. In fact, there are cases where you may not want to claim full CCA. Assume your business is losing money. Previous losses have already been used to obtain refunds in prior years. In this case it may make sense not to claim CCA. Save the deduction for future years.

Tax Beater

Delay claiming CCA in times where you may lose the use of the deduction.

Remember the "Tax Rate Stairway," careful planning to maximize lower tax levels may involve deferring your CCA claim. However, care should be taken with this type of planning. If you don't claim CCA in one year, you cannot double up your CCA claim in the next year. You are always limited to the maximum rate for that class.

Therefore, deferring CCA will just place you one year behind in depreciating the assets of that class.

For maximum flexibility and tax savings it is always wise, if you're considering deferring a CCA claim, to start by deferring the write-off of fast-depreciating assets first. For example, computer software is depreciated at the fast rate of 100%, but subject to the half-rate rule. Therefore, 50% is depreciated in the first year and 50% in the second year. If you defer claiming CCA on the computer software, you will be able to claim 100% of the CCA in the second or later year. This provides you with the maximum flexibility to manipulate your income, save tax dollars, and "Beat the Taxman."

Tax Beater

When deferring CCA deductions, start by deferring fast-depreciating assets first to provide maximum flexibility.

Is There a Right Time of the Year to Purchase Assets?

In many cases, the needs of your business will dictate when it is necessary to purchase a particular asset. However, if you have sufficient flexibility to time the purchase of a capital asset to maximize your tax savings, the best time to purchase assets from an income tax point of view is at the end of the business year. If the year-end of your business is December, you can obtain maximum tax savings by purchasing the asset in December as opposed to January of the next year.

By purchasing the depreciable asset at the end of the business year, you are speeding up the claiming of the CCA. The amount of CCA will not change, but you can claim it more quickly. Assume you have a December year-end and you are contemplating purchasing that (same old) computer for $3,000. It is now December, 1996, and you're debating whether to buy it before Christmas or after Christmas, in January of 1997. From an income tax point of view, purchasing the computer in December will provide the maximum tax savings since in the current

Tax Beater

Purchase assets at the end of the business year instead of the beginning of the next year.

year you would be able to claim $450 in CCA ($3,000 x 30% x ½) and then, in the next year, you would be able to claim $765 in CCA ($3,000 – $450 = $2,550 x 30%). Despite the fact that you purchased the computer in the last month of the year, you are still eligible to claim one-half of the year's CCA.

Alternatively, if you wait until January, 1997, to purchase your computer, you would have to wait until December of 1997 to claim any CCA on the computer. In that year you could claim $450 in CCA and then, not until the following year, or 1998, could you claim the $765 in CCA. By delaying the purchase by one month, you delay the timing of the tax savings by one full year.

In order to claim CCA on new purchases, it is important to ensure that the asset is available-for-use. Assuming your year-end is December, you can't pay for the computer in December, 1996, and have it delivered in January, 1997, and still be able to claim CCA in December, 1996. Despite the fact that you have paid for the computer, it is not available-for-use at your year-end since you didn't take possession of the computer until January.

It is important to realize that there is a difference between available-for-use and use. Maybe you don't have a need for that computer until February or March and you don't turn it on until then. You would still be eligible to claim CCA as long as you could have used the computer in December. Available-for-use does not mean you actually have to use it.

Tax Beater

Ensure that your capital purchase is available-for-use by the end of your business year, even if you don't, in fact, use it.

Is There a Right Time to Sell Capital Assets?

As a general rule, from a tax point of view, it is best to defer the sale of assets until the beginning of your next business year. When you sell a capital asset, you reduce the balance of the class by the lesser of the original cost of the asset or the proceeds received on disposing of the asset. By reducing the balance in the class, you also reduce the amount of CCA you can claim in a year.

Assume that you are looking to sell our old friend, the computer, for proceeds of $2,000. Assume also that the balance in class 10 at the end of the year is $10,000, due to the purchase of other assets over the years. If you dispose of the computer in December, your year-end, the maximum CCA you can claim is $2,400 ($10,000 – $2,000 x 30%). On the other hand, if you wait until January to sell that computer, the maximum CCA for the current year would be $3,000 ($10,000 x 30%). By delaying the sale by one month, you have increased your tax deductions by $600, which could amount to a $300 tax savings.

A critic would say that, yes, you get a greater deduction, but eventually it will catch up to you and you will have less of a CCA claim in a year due to this planning. And they would be right. But eventually could be a long time, depending on new purchases and other activities. And besides, as discussed previously, effective tax planning is deferring as long as possible the payment of tax. Even if the deferral is only for one year, it is better to pay tax next year than right now.

Tax Beater

If near your year-end, delay the sale of a capital asset until early the next year.

How Can I Save Tax Dollars With Capital Assets?

Not all capital purchases are treated equally. The faster an asset can be written off, the faster the tax savings can be realized on the purchase. The importance of properly identifying what class a capital asset belongs to and how it should be treated cannot be over-emphasized. Misclassifying capital additions can delay for years the tax savings you could otherwise have enjoyed. The following are some of the more common small and home-based business capital asset purchases that are treated uniquely.

Tax Beater

When purchasing a computer and software at the same time, break out the software portion of the purchase and deduct at the 100% CCA rate.

Computer Software

Computer software that you purchase (other than system software, the internal software previously installed on your computer) is eligible to be written off at the fast rate of 100%, subject to the half-rate rule. Software is included in class 12. It is important to break out the software you purchase at the same time as the computer, and not include the whole purchase price as computer equipment, which is deductible at 30%.

Electronic Office Equipment

With computers and electronic equipment becoming outdated at increasingly rapid rates, there is a tendency to replace this equipment faster than it is depreciated. This can result in the unenviable position of depreciating assets you don't own. For example, consider the purchase of our $3,000 computer. After two years you decide that this machine is just too slow, so you purchase another machine and sell the old one for $200. The old machine would have depreciated only to $1,785 after two years of maximum CCA. Since you purchased a new machine which is added to the class, you would not normally be able to claim the loss in value from $1,785 to $200 in the current year. Instead, you would continue to claim CCA at 30% on the balance in the class 10 pool. This results in a slow depreciation of the old computer which you don't own anymore.

To alleviate this problem, the government will allow you to place certain electronic office equipment into separate classes. The type of office equipment that will qualify for this treatment includes computers, fax machines, photocopiers, and telephone equipment. How the system works is instead of adding the fax machine to all of the other equipment in class 8 or the computer with all of the other assets in class 10, you create a separate class 8 and class 10 as appropriate for each piece of electronic office equipment purchased. The CCA rate for the separate class will be the same as the normal class, but by placing the asset in a separate class, you can claim a terminal loss on the equipment if you sell it early at a loss. For example, assume the above computer purchase had been allocated to a separate class 10. The CCA rate is still 30% subject to the half-rate rule in the first year. But in year three, if the asset is sold for $200, then the loss of $1,585 ($1,785 balance remaining in the separate class 10 minus the $200 proceeds on the sale) would be fully deductible in the current year.

In order to take advantage of this rule, the capital asset must be purchased after April 26, 1993, must have cost more than $1,000, and you must elect to treat the addition in this manner when you file your tax return for the year you purchased the equipment. To elect to treat the addition in this manner, just attach a note to Revenue Canada stating that you elect to include the electronic office equipment that you purchased in the current year in a separate class. If you still own the equipment after five years, the separate class must be added to the remaining pool.

Tax Beater

Elect to include electronic office equipment in a separate CCA class to potentially increase your tax deductions on sale.

Small Tools

Small tools that cost less than $200 are treated as class 12 asset additions not subject to the half-rate rule. This means that small tools costing less than $200 each can be fully expensed in the current year. If a tool costs more than $200, unless it falls under a different class, it will need to be added to class 8 and depreciated at 20% per year.

Remember, this rule is looked at on an individual tool-by-tool basis. If you purchase more than one tool, the invoice may be greater than $200. However, as long as the individual tools are less than $200 each, they should qualify for the 100% write-off.

Tax Beater

Deduct 100% of the cost of tools costing less than $200.

Can I Deduct the Cost of a Personal Asset Which Is Now Being Used in the Business?

If you start using a personal capital asset in your business, you can deduct capital cost allowance on that capital asset. When you begin using a personal asset in the business, there is a deemed change in use of that asset. It no longer is consider a personal asset, but is instead considered a business asset.

Tax Beater

Deduct CCA on personal assets which are now being used in your business.

As a result of the change in use, you are considered to have sold the asset to your business. Even though no cash will trade hands, you are treated as if the "personal you" sold it to the "business you." In most cases, the value you place on the asset will be its fair market value at the time of the change in use. In other words, the value you would use as an addition to the CCA schedule is the value you would pay if you were purchasing the same asset from a stranger.

For example, assume you have just started the business and the business is going to use your personal computer. The cost of the computer was $3,000, but today it is worth only $1,000. You would add $1,000 to class 10 for the value of the computer. The difference between $3,000 and $1,000 is not deductible, since this decrease in value occurred while the computer was owned by you personally.

If you change the use of an asset that has gone up in value, the calculation can be somewhat more complicated. Your starting point is the same, that is, estimating the fair market value of the asset. However, you must deduct from that any capital gains exemption claimed on that property, but only to the point that it may reduce the fair market value down to the original cost. In addition, you may have to report a capital gain on the transfer of the property.

For example, assume that you are going to turn your cottage into a fishing store and boat rental office. On your 1994 income tax return, you used the capital gains exemption on that cottage in the amount of $20,000 ($7,000 related to the land and $13,000 related to the building). The land originally cost $10,000 and the building $50,000. The value of the cottage is now estimated at $100,000 (land value $20,000 and building value $80,000). The amount that you could add to your CCA building class would be $67,000, that is, $80,000 minus the capital gains exemption on the building of $13,000.

You will also have to report a capital gain on this change in use of the cottage. Since you are considered to have sold your cottage at its fair market value when you turn it into a business property, you will have to pay tax on any increase in value in the property. In this case, the capital gain on the total property would be $20,000. See the chart below for details on how this is calculated.

Calculation of Capital Gain	Building	Land	Total
	$	$	$
Cost	50	10	60
Elected capital gain	13	7	20
	63	17	80
Fair Market Value Now	80	20	100
Capital Gain	17	3	20
Calculation of Addition to CCA Class			
Fair Market Value	80	* N/A	80
Less Elected Capital Gain	13	N/A	13
Eligible Addition to CCA claim	67	N/A	67

* Cannot claim CCA on land

Can I Claim CCA on Assets Used Only Part of the Time in My Business?

When assets are used part of the time in your business and part of the time personally, you can still claim CCA on the asset. However, you are restricted in how much you can claim, based

Tax Beater

Deduct a portion of the cost of assets used both personally and in a business.

on a reasonable estimate of how long the asset was used for business purposes. For example, assume the computer is used part of the time in the business and it is also used by the kids for homework and video games. And let's say you estimate that the business use is about 60% of the total time the computer is being used. To calculate how much CCA can be claimed in the business, first calculate the maximum amount of CCA that can be claimed on the computer. In our example above it was $450 in the first year. Multiply that by 60%. The remaining 40% is not tax deductible.

Should I Claim CCA on My Personal Residence?

In most cases your tax coach would not recommend claiming CCA on your house for the single reason that when you go to sell your home, you may find yourself paying some tax. Normally when you sell your home, you don't have to pay any tax on the increase in value of the home because of an exemption called the "principal residence exemption." If you convert 10% of your home into an office and you claim 10% of the CCA available on the cost of your home, then when you go to sell, 10% of any increase in value will be taxable as a capital gain. In addition, when you do sell your home, you will have to include in your income, and pay tax on, the CCA that you had claimed over the years. In most cases the tax deduction is just not worth the extra tax you may have to pay.

Claiming CCA may make sense where you have more than one personal residence, like a cottage, and you were not planning to use the principal residence exemption on your home that has the office. Or, you are really sure that your home will not be sold at a profit.

What Is an Eligible Capital Expenditure?

An eligible capital expenditure is a type of expenditure that doesn't really fit as a depreciable expenditure, nor can it be reasonably expensed in the current year. Eligible capital expenditures are often referred to as "nothings" or "intangibles" because the expenditure is for something that can't be seen or felt. A good example is goodwill you purchase when buying an existing business. The goodwill typically represents the positive name of the business in the community, good employee morale, excellent customer relations, and so on. It is often because of the goodwill built up in a business that you are willing to pay more for it. Another example of an eligible capital expenditure is the cost of an unlimited life franchise or licence. These expenditures are certainly valuable, but you can't point to them and say here is what I purchased.

Another common eligible capital expenditure is legal and accounting fees spent to incorporate a business. Revenue Canada considers these expenses to have a long-term benefit; therefore, they are not a current expense. On the other hand, there is no CCA class that could handle professional fees spent to incorporate a business. Accordingly, these fees fall into the category of eligible capital expenditures.

Can I Deduct Eligible Capital Expenditures?

You can deduct eligible capital expenditures, but like depreciable expenditures, you can deduct them only over time. However, unlike depreciable expenditures, you can deduct only three-quarters of an eligible capital expenditure.

Three-quarters of all eligible capital expenditures that you purchase for your business are added to one pool. Each year you can deduct 7% of the balance in that pool. As you can see, it will take a long time to deduct an eligible capital expenditure.

Can I Deduct My Own Goodwill?

I am often asked: If goodwill is an eligible capital expenditure, can I deduct the goodwill that I have created in my business? Unfortunately, the answer to this is no. You can deduct only the goodwill that you have purchased from someone else.

Am I Taxed on the Goodwill I Sell?

When you sell your business, if a portion of the purchase price is allocated to goodwill, then you will be taxed on the sale of that goodwill. However, you will be taxed on only three-quarters of the goodwill you sell, just as you were only able to deduct three-quarters of the goodwill you purchased.

Can I Reduce the Potential Tax Liability on the Sale of Goodwill?

If you were operating your business as a sole proprietor or as a partnership on February 22, 1994, it may be possible to shelter from tax some of the goodwill that you have generated.

On February 22, 1994, the federal government did away with the $100,000 capital gains exemption on other property. However, they allowed you to elect on property that you owned at that time to make use of the capital gains exemption. This election allowed you to pretend to sell property at its fair value and then turn around and buy it back. This process allowed you to make use of your eligible capital gains exemption and thereby save tax in the future. Cottage property and shares held on the stock market received a lot of press. But using the capital gains exemption on goodwill generated in a sole proprietorship or partnership did not receive very much attention. Goodwill that you created could be elected—to potentially reduce the tax burden on the sale of your business by thousands of dollars.

The election was supposed to be filed by April 30, 1995, or

April 30, 1996, depending on the year-end of your business. However, there are provisions to file the election
late for up to two years after the filing deadline for your
business. If you file the election late, you will have to
pay a penalty; however, depending on your situation,
the penalty may be worth the potential tax savings
down the road.

If you believe that you have significant goodwill
built up in your business before February 22, 1994, and
you did not use up all of your $100,000 capital gains
exemption, it may be worthwhile investigating this further. It could mean significant tax savings.

Tax Beater

Consider late-filing
the $100,000 capital
gains election on
built up goodwill.
You could save
thousands of dollars.

AUTO-matic Savings

Most entrepreneurs want to deduct the costs of operating an automobile used in their business. And rightly so. Deducting automobile costs is very important in reducing your tax liability. It is one of the tax deductions that I am frequently asked about and ranks right up there with home-office expenses in importance. It is also, unfortunately, one of the more complex areas for small businesses, with many rules and restrictions. However, knowing these rules and planning your affairs accordingly can provide you with significant tax savings and will ensure that you win Round 10.

What Automobile Expenses Can I Deduct?

As a general rule, you can deduct any expense incurred to operate your vehicle. This includes the gas and oil to run the vehicle, the maintenance and repairs to keep the vehicle on the road, the licence and registration fees, the insurance costs, leasing costs or capital cost allowance, and interest costs if you purchase the vehicle.

If you use your vehicle strictly for business purposes, you will be eligible to deduct 100% of the motor vehicle expenses. However, in many cases the vehicle is used for both business and personal use. In this case, you are eligible to deduct only those automobile expenses that relate to the business. To determine how much of an expense is eligible to be deducted, divide your total business kilometres in a year by the total kilometres driven and multiply this by your automobile expenses.

For example, assume that your automobile expenses amounted to $3,000 in the year and your business kilometres equalled 15,000 kilometres. Your total annual driving was 20,000 kilometres. The amount you can deduct on your tax return for automobile expenses would be:

$$\$3,000 \ \times \ \frac{15,000 \ (\text{business kilometres})}{20,000 \ (\text{total kilometres})} \ = \ \$2,250$$

To ensure that you can obtain the maximum tax deduction for your vehicle, make sure you keep all receipts to support your automobile expenses and that you keep some sort of log or record of your business kilometres. Remember, if you are challenged on your tax deductions, it is up to you to prove that your deduction is reasonable.

Tax Beater

Record all business kilometres you drive.

Revenue Canada suggests that you keep a log for all of your business trips, which includes the date of the trip, destination, purpose, and number of kilometres driven. Unfortunately, not everyone is disciplined enough to keep such a log. What happens is that you forget business kilometres and don't claim them, or Revenue Canada reduces your claim since there is no support for the business kilometres.

If keeping a log is not for you, consider this trick. If you carry an appointment book around with you, write down beside the appointment the number of kilometres driven. Include in your appointment book business errands you have to run and write the kilometres driven for those. At the end of the month add up the kilometres driven and write that down in the back of the book. With this method you have the date and approximate time the driving occurred, you have the kilometres driven, you have the customer name, and possibly the purpose of the trip. You will have all the information needed without having to keep separate logs.

Remember that you can have more than one personal vehicle that is used in your business. If you use two or more vehicles interchangeably, keep track of all auto expenses for both vehicles and then divide the number of business kilometres by the total kilometres for both vehicles to arrive at the amount of automotive expenses that can be deducted.

If you have two personal vehicles at home and you need only one, you may want to consider using the vehicle with the most operating costs in the business. If one vehicle is paid for and does not require any maintenance, whereas the other vehicle still has a loan outstanding, requires more maintenance, and is less fuel efficient, you can increase your tax deductions by using the second vehicle in your business. This especially makes sense if both vehicles are being driven about the same number of kilometres per year.

At the year-end of your business, remember to record the odometer reading on the vehicles you are using in your business. If this is your first year of operation or if you are just beginning to claim auto expenses, remember to record the odometer reading at the beginning of your business year or from the point that you are beginning to use the vehicle in the business.

Tax Beater

Keep all automotive receipts to support your tax deduction.

Tax Beater

If two or more vehicles are used in your business, keep track of the business kilometres on each vehicle to maximize your tax deductions.

Tax Beater

Maximize tax savings by using the vehicle with higher operating costs.

Tax Beater

Record your odometer readings at the beginning and end of each year.

The odometer reading is important to calculate the overall kilometres driven in your business's fiscal year. If you estimate this number, you may estimate too high, which will reduce the amount of auto expenses you can claim as a tax deduction.

As a self-employed owner of a business, you are not allowed to simply take a per kilometre charge and deduct this as an auto expense. You must keep your receipts relating to your automobile and deduct the actual costs. The per kilometre allowance is reserved for your employees if you reimburse them for auto expenses incurred on business. As an owner of your sole proprietorship, you cannot be considered an employee and would therefore not be eligible for a per-kilometre allowance.

What Is Considered "Business Travel"?

Travelling on business includes any reasonable travelling you conduct to and from your customer's place of business or in the performance of your business. This includes travelling to the store or to a different city to purchase business supplies, travelling to meet a client to conduct business, or travelling to and from a business conference or course.

Tax Beater

Schedule client meetings on the way to and from work to increase business kilometres and save taxes.

However, if you have an office away from your home, travelling to and from your office would not be considered business travelling. This is personal. On the other hand, if your office is at home and a client provides you an office on a temporary basis to conduct business, travelling back and forth to that office would usually be considered business travelling.

If you do have an office away from your home, a legitimate way to increase your business kilometres is to schedule meetings with clients on the way to and from work. This will turn a non-deductible personal trip into a fully deductible business trip.

Can I Deduct the Cost of My Car in the Business?

As we have already stated, you can deduct the cost of your vehicle in the business, subject to certain restrictions, provided it is used for business purposes. However, a vehicle is considered a capital asset and therefore can only be deducted over time in the form of capital cost allowance. (See Round 9 for more details on capital assets.) As well, you can deduct only the portion of the capital cost allowance that relates to business use. Follow the same rules to calculate what the maximum capital cost allowance would be for the year by multiplying the CCA amount by the number of business kilometres over the total kilometres driven, but beware, there are special rules (I warned you this was a complex area!).

If the vehicle was purchased after September 1, 1989, and cost less than $24,000 ($20,000 if purchased between June 17, 1987, and August 31, 1989), then there would be no other restrictions beyond that stated in the previous paragraph. The vehicle would be considered a class 10 asset and eligible for a 30% CCA rate, subject to the half-rate rule in the year of purchase.

If the cost of the vehicle is greater than $24,000 before GST and any provincial sales tax, as applicable, then an additional restriction may apply to reduce the amount of CCA that may be claimed. If the vehicle is considered to be a passenger vehicle, you will be restricted in how much of the cost of the vehicle you can deduct in your business.

The intention of the legislation is to reduce the amount that could be deducted in a business on expensive luxury vehicles. The government has set a threshold of $24,000 plus GST and PST on purchases of vehicles after December 31, 1990. If you purchase a passenger vehicle that costs more than $24,000, you will only be able to add $24,000 plus the applicable GST and PST on to your CCA schedule. If you are eligible to claim GST input tax credits you will not be able to add the GST to your CCA schedule.

A separate CCA class, class 10.1, is reserved for each vehicle purchase that exceeds the $24,000 threshold. With class 10.1 come some peculiar tax treatments. For example, only one vehicle is added to each 10.1 class. Therefore, if you have two passenger vehicles you are using in your business that exceed the $24,000 threshold, you will have two class 10.1 entries on your CCA schedule.

If you sell a class 10.1 vehicle, despite the fact that there is only one asset in the class, you will not be allowed to claim a *terminal loss* or to include *recapture* in your income. In Round 9 I showed how, when the last asset of a class was sold, you could claim a terminal loss or recapture on your tax return. However, with class 10.1 assets, no terminal loss or recapture is allowed. Instead, you can claim one-half of the normal CCA you would have been able to claim on the vehicle had you still owned it at the year-end. The balance remaining in the class 10.1 pool just disappears.

With a class 10.1 vehicle, the cost of the vehicle that is in excess of the $24,000 threshold never gets deducted for tax purposes. This is obviously not a desirable result. Where possible, you should take steps to reduce the effect of this limitation.

One way to maximize your tax deductions is to review what types of vehicles are considered passenger vehicles and what types are not. For example, a minivan that is used more than 50% of the time to transport goods and equipment, and that cannot accommodate more than the driver and two passengers, would not be considered a passenger vehicle. Therefore, even if the minivan cost $40,000, it would be an eligible class 10 asset and depreciated in the business subject to the normal business use restrictions. On the other hand, a minivan that can accommodate more than three passengers would be considered a passenger vehicle, unless it is used to transport goods, equipment or passengers for more than 90% of the time in the business. The following "Vehicle Definition" chart may be helpful for deciding which class your vehicle belongs to.

VEHICLE DEFINITIONS

Type of Vehicle	Seating (includes driver)	Business use in year bought or leased	Vehicle definition
Coupe, sedan, station wagon, sports or luxury car	1 to 9	1% to 100%	passenger
Pick-up truck used to transport goods or equipment	1 to 3	more than 50%	motor
Pick-up truck (other than above)	1 to 3	1% to 100%	passenger
Pick-up truck with extended cab used to transport goods, equipment or passengers	4 to 9	90% or more	motor
Pick-up truck with extended cab (other than above)	4 to 9	1% to 100%	passenger
Sport utility used to transport goods, equipment or passengers	4 to 9	90% or more	motor
Sport utility (other than above)	4 to 9	1% to 100%	passenger
Van or minivan used to transport goods or equipment	1 to 3	more than 50%	motor
Van or minivan (other than above)	1 to 3	1% to 100%	passenger
Van or minivan used to transport goods, equipment or passengers	4 to 9	90% or more	motor
Van or minivan (other than above)	4 to 9	1% to 100%	passenger

Source: Revenue Canada

Another way to maximize your tax deductions is by negotiating a good deal on your vehicle purchase. If you can negotiate a lower price for your vehicle by possibly accepting less on your trade-in, you might be able to avoid the class 10.1 treatment. For example, let's say you are considering purchasing a $25,000 vehicle which would normally be considered a passenger vehicle and you are trading in a vehicle which may be worth $12,000. The dealership is going to receive $13,000 cash after the trade-in. So if you could negotiate a purchase price of only $23,000 for the new vehicle and accept, say, $10,000 for the trade-in, then you could avoid the class 10.1 restrictions. Since the dealership will still get their $13,000 cash, they may be willing to help you out.

Tax Beater

Avoid class 10.1 restrictions by negotiating favourable new vehicle purchase deals.

Of course, Revenue Canada could argue that the trade-in value was too low and adjust the deal. However, by having the invoice structured in your favour at the beginning, it will provide you with the support to make the claim. Also, the transaction is between two parties operating as strangers to each other. In all but the most obviously aggressive situations, the invoice will likely stand and you will be able to avoid the class 10.1 restrictions.

Are There Any Restrictions on Lease Costs?

Yes. You can't get around the class 10.1 restrictions by leasing a vehicle. Similar restrictions are in place to limit on an annual basis the amount of lease costs which may be deducted in your business. The lease restriction rules are very complex. Their intent is to equalize the benefits to an individual who purchases a vehicle and an individual who leases a vehicle.

Generally, the lease restriction is calculated as the lesser of two calculations. The first calculation is as follows:

$$\frac{\$650 \text{ (plus GST and PST as applicable) x \# of days the vehicle was leased from the beginning of the lease}}{30} - \begin{array}{c} \text{lease payments} \\ \text{deducted in} \\ \text{prior years} \end{array}$$

The second calculation is:

$$\frac{\$24,000 \text{ (plus GST and PST as applicable) x actual lease charges in the year}}{.85 \text{ x greater of i) manufacturer's list price plus the PST that would be charged,}}$$

or

ii) $28,235 plus GST and PST on $28,235 as applicable

You are allowed to deduct the lesser of these two calculations. These formulas are based on a lease that was started after

January 1, 1991. If the lease began before January 1, 1991, you should contact Revenue Canada for the previous prescribed amounts. In addition, these formulas will become more complex if you make a refundable deposit on the lease and if you receive reimbursements.

Generally speaking, if your lease costs are less than $650 per month, then you should not fall into the above restrictions. One way to ensure that your lease costs are kept low is to structure your lease agreement to exclude insurance, repairs, maintenance, and licences. If these costs are included, consider requesting that they be valued and broken out of the agreement. Where these costs are included in the lease payments, you must include the costs in the above restrictions.

Tax Beater

Maximize your lease deduction by keeping operating expenses out of the lease agreement.

Can I Deduct All Interest Charges on My Vehicle?

You can deduct interest paid to finance the purchase of a vehicle to the extent that the vehicle is used for business purposes. However, if the vehicle is considered a passenger vehicle, you will be limited to claiming up to a maximum of $10 per day interest on the vehicle. At the end of the year, you can claim the lesser of the actual interest paid or $10 per day times the number of days that interest was paid. The lesser of these two numbers will still be restricted by the pro-ration of business use over total use.

When borrowing money to purchase a passenger vehicle, it is wise to keep this interest restriction in mind. If you can arrange your affairs so that the interest will not exceed the maximum by using excess cash to finance the balance of the purchase price, you will maximize your tax savings.

Tax Beater

Arrange new car financing so that none of the interest is restricted.

Should I Own My Passenger Vehicle in My Corporation?

A frequently asked question is whether to own your car personally or in the corporation. There are several schools of thought on this and ultimately the decision will depend on your individual situation. However, if you like things simple, my advice is to own the car personally.

Over the years, the government has worked hard to remove the benefit of having personal use vehicles owned by a corporation. The corporation is subject to the same restrictions on capital cost allowance and lease costs as an individual. In addition, you will need to calculate and add to your T4 a taxable benefit referred to as a *standby charge* for the use of that vehicle.

The standby charge can be a very significant cost. If the vehicle is owned by the company and not used in the business at least 90% of the time or more, the standby charge is equal to 2% times the original cost of the vehicle (excluding GST, but including provincial sales tax, for cars purchased before 1992) for each month the vehicle was available for your use. Note that the original cost is not limited by the $24,000 threshold amount. Therefore, your company may only be able to deduct $24,000 plus GST and PST as applicable, yet you will be assessed a standby charge on the full original value of the vehicle.

If the vehicle is leased, the standby charge is equal to two thirds of the lease cost of the vehicle, including any maintenance and repair costs included in the lease, but not including insurance. As is the case when the company owns the vehicle, the lease standby charge is calculated on the full lease cost, not the restricted amount allowed as a deduction to the company.

In addition, if the company pays all of the operating costs on the vehicle, i.e., gas, oil, maintenance and repairs, insurance, etc., you will also have to add to your T4 a taxable benefit for these operating expenses. This taxable benefit is calculated by multiplying 12 cents by the number of personal kilometres in the year. If the vehicle is used at least 50% of the time for business purposes, you have the option of including 50% of the standby charge as a taxable benefit.

If the vehicle is used 90% of the time or more in the business and your personal use is less than 1,000 kilometres per month, the standby charge can be significantly reduced. The following equation shows how this reduction works:

$$\text{Standby charge otherwise calculated} \times \frac{\text{Kilometres for personal use in the year}}{1{,}000 \times \text{number of months in the year in which the car was available}}$$

If, for example, your personal kilometres averaged out to 100 kilometres per month and the vehicle was used at least 90% of the time for business use, you would only have to include 10% (1,200 km/12,000) of the standby charge in your income. This reduction applies equally whether the vehicle is leased or purchased.

Tax Beater

Own your personal vehicle personally instead of in a corporation.

If only 10% of the standby charge is being included in income, it may make sense to have the corporation own your vehicle. However, if you can't meet the 90% business usage test, in most cases you're better off to own the vehicle personally.

How Can I Reduce the Amount of the Standby Charge?

If your vehicle is in the company and you don't want to change this structure, you may be able to take some action to reduce the standby charge.

If your personal kilometres are relatively low, consider calculating your operating expense taxable benefit using the 12 cents per personal kilometre method rather than the easier

Tax Beater

When personal kilometres are low, use the 12 cents per personal kilometre method of calculating your operating taxable benefit.

Tax Beater

Before purchasing your vehicle, compare the standby charge under the lease option.

Tax Beater

Reduce your standby charge by selling your vehicle to one of your other operating companies.

method of just taking 50% of the standby charge. This will mean that you will have to keep track of your business or personal kilometres, but it may save you tax dollars over the long run.

Another way to reduce your standby charge is to keep track of when the vehicle is not available for your use. For example, keep track of when you're out of town and you don't have access to your car. If you take another family vehicle on vacations, exclude that time in the calculation of standby charge.

Another way you might reduce the standby charge is to compare the charge for a leased and purchased vehicle. You may find that including two thirds of the lease costs will be less expensive than 24% of the purchase cost.

One last trick to "Beat the Taxman" is to consider selling your vehicle to another one of your companies. If you have more than one operating company, consider selling the used vehicle to one of your other companies at its true fair market value. Remember, the standby charge is calculated at the rate of 2% per month times the original cost of the vehicle. If that vehicle cost you $50,000 five years ago, you will still be calculating a standby charge based on $50,000. It may only be worth $20,000 now. If that's the case, sell the vehicle to one of your other companies for $20,000. The standby charge will then be calculated at the lower purchase price.

One word of caution. The other company should be earning income of a type that would substantiate a vehicle expense. Otherwise, operating expenses and capital cost allowance would be denied in that company because they were not incurred for the purpose of earning income.

If I Own My Car Personally, How Should the Company Reimburse Me for Business Travelling?

If you have decided to own your car personally, but you use the vehicle for business travel, your corporation can reimburse you. You can structure this two ways. You can provide expense reports to the company on a periodic basis, detailing the business kilometres travelled, and receive a reasonable reimbursement on a per-kilometre basis. Alternatively, you can receive a reasonable tax-free allowance for business travel.

Revenue Canada views a reasonable reimbursement on a per-kilometre basis to be equal to 33 cents per kilometre for the first 5,000 kilometres and 27 cents per kilometre thereafter. (Note that an additional 4 cents per kilometre is allowed if travelling in the Yukon or Northwest Territories.) A reasonable allowance is viewed by Revenue Canada as an allowance that is based on a per-business-kilometre rate and you are not receiving any other reimbursements for business travelling.

If the allowance or reimbursement is considered reasonable, then the allowance will not be taxable in your hands. If the allowance is based on a per-kilometre charge and you do not receive any other reimbursements, but Revenue Canada considers the allowance to be unreasonably high, the excess will be included in your income as a taxable benefit.

If the allowance is not based on a per-kilometre charge or you receive other reimbursements, the full allowance will be included in your income. However, you will then be allowed to deduct from that the actual costs to operate your vehicle for business purposes.

Overall, if your business is incorporated, it is generally easier and more cost effective to own your vehicle personally and pay yourself a reasonable tax-free car allowance.

Tax Beater

Save time and money: pay yourself a reasonable tax-free car allowance on personally owned vehicles.

ROUND ELEVEN

Saving by Spending

The government, from time to time, will attempt to stimulate a particular segment of the economy by offering what is referred to as investment tax credits. As you spend money to purchase equipment for your business, you can save significant tax dollars if you can make use of these tax credits.

Investment tax credits are becoming less popular with cash-strapped governments and we are finding that many of the programs that were available have now been reduced or eliminated. However, there are a couple of lucrative programs still around and you may be eligible to apply for past programs giving you that one-two combination to win this Round.

What Is an Investment Tax Credit?

Investment tax credits provide a reduction in your tax liability based on a set percentage of qualified purchases. For example, if you purchased some equipment for $200 that qualified for an

Tax Beater

Reduce the tax you pay with investment tax credits.

ITC rebate of 20%, you could reduce the amount of tax you pay to the government by $40.

Most ITCs relate to the purchase of manufacturing and processing equipment, fishing and farming equipment, certain types of transportation and construction equipment, and research and development expenditures. If your business purchases do not fall into these categories, it is very likely that you will not be eligible for an investment tax credit. Since governments are trying to encourage specific industries and activities, ITCs are not for everyone.

Who Can Claim Investment Tax Credits?

Investment tax credits can be claimed by individuals, partners in a partnership, or corporations. In order to claim investment tax credits you must be engaged in an activity or purchasing equipment in an area that will allow you the credit. For example, anyone who is involved in Scientific Research and Experimental Development (SR&ED) anywhere in Canada is eligible to claim an investment tax credit on their expenditures. As well, anyone who lives in the maritime provinces or the Gaspé Peninsula region of Quebec may be eligible for an investment tax credit on certain capital purchases made for their businesses.

In order to qualify for the investment tax credit in the maritime provinces or the Gaspé Peninsula region of Quebec (other than under the SR&ED program), the asset purchased must be new, and used in Canada primarily in an activity prescribed by the government, such as manufacturing or processing goods for sale or lease, farming, fishing, logging, storing grain, and producing industrial minerals.

If you live in the far north of Canada, you were eligible for an investment tax credit on the purchase of certain capital expenditures made before January 1, 1995. If there was a written agreement to commit you to a purchase after January 1,

1995, and the agreement was signed on or before February 22, 1994, then you still may be eligible for this very lucrative 30% investment tax credit. As well, if you missed claiming this ITC, it would be worth discussing with Revenue Canada the possibility of amending your tax return.

If you lived anywhere in Canada and purchased certain types of manufacturing, farming, fishing, construction, or transportation property between December 2, 1992, and January 1, 1994, you were eligible for a 10% investment tax credit. This investment tax credit program has not been in operation since 1993. However, if you feel you may have had a purchase in 1993 that would have qualified for this tax credit, as a sole proprietor or a member of a partnership you are still eligible to go back and apply for a refund. In circumstances where you have missed claiming a tax credit, you can in fact apply for a refund back to 1985.

Deciding what purchases qualify for investment tax credits is not an easy task. So if you feel you may have purchased some assets that would qualify for an investment tax credit, discuss it with your tax coach or contact Revenue Canada. The potential tax savings is worth the time.

Tax Beater

Amend prior year tax returns to save on forgotten investment tax credits.

How Do I Claim an Investment Tax Credit?

If you are eligible to claim an investment tax credit for a purchase other than for scientific research and experimental development, all you will need to do is complete Form T2038 (IND), "Investment Tax Credit (Individuals) 1995 and Subsequent Years" and submit it with your completed tax return. With this form you will be able to calculate the amount of tax credit available by multiplying the cost of the purchase by the investment tax credit rate. You may then deduct this investment tax credit from taxes you would otherwise have to pay.

Tax Beater

Apply for 40% investment tax credit refund to speed up tax savings.

Tax Beater

Apply unused investment tax credits to past and future taxation years.

Tax Beater

Reduce CCA claims to use up investment tax credits before they expire.

Tax Beater

File your tax return on time to ensure ITC carry backs are accepted by Revenue Canada.

If after deducting the eligible investment tax credit from your tax liability, there is still a balance left over, you may apply to have up to 40% of the balance refunded in the current year. Most investment tax credit programs offer this refundable feature. However, the investment tax credits that were available between the period of December 2, 1992, and December 31, 1993, were referred to as non-refundable investment tax credits and were not eligible for the 40% refund.

If there is still a balance left over, the balance can be carried back three years to reduce tax liabilities, or forward ten years. This system should provide ample opportunity to make use of the investment tax credits. As a planning point, if it appears that investment tax credits may start to be lost, you should consider reducing discretionary expenses like not claiming CCA or not providing for receivables.

Note that the request to have an investment tax credit applied to a previous year must be made with the filing of your tax return in the year the investment tax credit arose. If your tax return is filed late that year, Revenue Canada has the authority not to accept the tax credit carry back. In most cases they will agree to carry the tax credit back, but if you file your tax return late, you run the risk of their saying no. It is another example of the importance of filing your tax return on time, even if you know you don't have a tax liability.

Investment tax credits are provided by the government as an incentive for you to make certain purchases. In effect, they are providing a rebate. Accordingly, that purchase didn't really cost you as much as you reported when you added it to the capital cost allowance schedule.

Recognizing this, the government requires you to reduce the balance in the capital cost allowance class by the amount of the investment tax credit refund you receive. You make the adjustment in the year after the year in which you reduce your income taxes. For example, say you purchase a $1,000 piece of equipment for manufacturing that is eligible for a 20% or $200 investment tax credit. When you purchased the equipment you would have added $1,000 to class 43, representing the cost of that equipment for that year. You applied for and will receive a refund of $200 as an investment tax credit. This $200 must be recorded as a reduction in class 43 next year. It will therefore reduce the amount of CCA claim that will be available in that year and future years.

What Expenditures Qualify For SR&ED?

One of the most lucrative incentive programs currently being offered in Canada is the Scientific Research and Experimental Development (SR&ED) program. To qualify under this program you must be engaged in an activity that qualifies as scientific research and experimental development. The income tax regulations define SR&ED as "a systematic investigation or search carried out in a field of science or technology by means of experiment or analysis." SR&ED includes:

- basic research that is engaged in just to further scientific knowledge, even though there may be no specific application of this knowledge
- applied research, which is research engaged to further scientific knowledge with a specific application in mind
- development, which includes applying this research to create something new or significantly improved.

So, basically, SR&ED includes research for the sake of research, research with a specific use in mind, and the development of a new and improved product. However, in order for an expenditure to qualify as SR&ED, the expenditure must be related to a business you are engaged in, the expenditure must be in the scientific or technology field, and the activity must happen in Canada.

Normally, in order to qualify there must be some uncertainty about the outcome of the work that you are doing. If you know beyond a shadow of a doubt that what you are creating will work, then you are not likely engaged in SR&ED.

Keep in mind also, that it is possible to be engaged in SR&ED activities if you have to reinvent the wheel, so to speak, for your business. Where a certain product or process is available only to a limited number of companies and you have to reinvent that product or process on your own, you may still qualify for SR&ED tax credits. However, if the technology is common knowledge, then your expenditures would not normally qualify.

SR&ED does not include research and development in any of the humanities or in product style changes. For example, market research, sales promotion, quality control, data collection, and ongoing style changes would not qualify for SR&ED. Nor would research and development for a new book or course qualify for the tax credit. The activity must be science-oriented and result in a technological improvement or advancement.

There is a fine line between routine enhancements of a product that would not qualify for SR&ED tax credits and a technological advancement that would qualify. Consider, for example, an ice cream maker that adds a new flavour to its list of ice cream flavours. Yes, research and development had to go into the creation of that new flavour. But the basic process is already established. It is just a matter of trying different ingredients until they get a tasty product.

On the other hand, consider the ice cream maker that, for the first time ever, developed frozen yogurt. Here is a product that may taste similar to ice cream but is significantly different. This is an advancement in technology for the ice cream business. The research and development that went into developing frozen yogurt for the first time should qualify for research and development. However, if the making of frozen yogurt is now common knowledge for those in the industry, a company developing their own brand of frozen yogurt would not qualify for SR&ED unless they are improving the technology somehow.

In many cases, it is difficult to determine if a certain activity will qualify for SR&ED. Unfortunately, Revenue Canada will not provide you with an advance ruling on whether or not a certain activity will qualify. However, they may provide you with an informal verbal suggestion as to whether you would be wasting your time applying for the tax credit or not. If you do decide to contact Revenue Canada, make sure you ask for someone working in the SR&ED department.

What are the Tax Benefits of Claiming SR&ED?

If you are engaged in SR&ED activities, you can enjoy several tax advantages and benefits. The tax benefits are a result of receiving very favourable tax treatments regarding deducting SR&ED expenditures as well as being eligible for investment tax credits on these expenditures.

Delay Deducting Expenses

All expenditures that relate to SR&ED activities are eligible to be included in a pool of expenditures. This includes both expense and capital expenditures. You can deduct this pool of expenditures basically whenever you want. For example, if you are incurring losses and you can't make use of additional losses, you can delay deducting the pool of expenditures. Usually, expense items must be deducted and added to your loss carry forward if your business is losing money. However, SR&ED expense items can be added to the pool and deducted when it suits your tax planning. This is especially important when you consider that business loss carry forwards have a limited seven year life, and then they expire.

Tax Beater

Delay deducting SR&ED expenses to reduce risk of loss carry forwards expiring.

Speed Up Deducting Capital Expenditures

With capital items, you are normally restricted to a slow depreciation of the expenditure over time. However, if the capital expenditure relates to SR&ED, you are eligible to expense the item all in one year. This again provides significant flexibility in planning your tax strategy and minimizing your taxes.

Tax Beater

Deduct SR&ED capital expenditures all in one year.

Claim 20% Investment Tax Credits

As mentioned earlier, SR&ED expenditures also qualify for investment tax credits. As an individual or member of a partnership, all SR&ED expenditures, whether capital or expense items, qualify for a 20% investment tax credit rate. (This rate used to be 30%, for individuals and members of a partnership that lived in the four Atlantic provinces or in the Gaspé Peninsula and if the expenditure was made before 1995.)

Claim 35% Investment Tax Credits

Tax Beater

Consider incorporating your business to receive an additional 15% investment tax credit.

If the SR&ED activities are engaged within a small Canadian corporation, the tax credit increases to 35%, up to a maximum of $2,000,000 in expenditures. If your business is heavily engaged in SR&ED activities, it may be worth considering incorporating your business, given the extra 15% investment tax credit available to small companies. However, the extra tax credit should be weighed against all the other pros and cons of incorporating as discussed in Round 5.

Claim 40% Refund of Investment Tax Credits

Another advantage of the SR&ED program is that the investment tax credits can be refunded, even if there is no tax liability. For individuals and partnerships, 40% of the investment tax credit not used to reduce the current year's income tax liability can be refunded on your personal tax return. The balance can then be carried back or forward to reduce past and future tax liabilities. The 40% refund provides a cash incentive even in a year where you would not normally be paying any tax.

Tax Beater

Claim your 40% refund of excess investment tax credits on your personal return.

Claim 100% Refund of Investment Tax Credits

For small corporations, the 40% refund of investment tax credits increases to 100%. In other words, despite the fact that a corporation may have no taxable income, they can still receive a refund of up to 100% of the investment tax credits calculated in the year. This provides another incentive to incorporate a business that is engaging in SR&ED.

Tax Beater

Consider incorporating your business to receive a 100% refund of investment tax credits.

How Do You Claim a SR&ED Tax Benefit?

In order to qualify for the favourable tax treatments under the SR&ED program, you must complete and submit to Revenue Canada form T661, "Claim for Scientific Research and Experimental Development Expenditures Carried on in Canada," in addition to the form T2038 discussed previously. If this is your first submission of a SR&ED project, Revenue Canada will request that an expert in your industry review your project confidentially to ensure that it meets the government guidelines for qualification. If the scientific expert approves the project, a Revenue Canada auditor will review the mathematical calculations of the claim. Once this is complete, the government will process the refunds.

If you have made previous submissions for SR&ED projects that have received approvals, then the process is normally streamlined or fast-tracked. Your first claim will be reviewed carefully, 100% of the time. My experience has been, however, that the auditors are very helpful and do not audit other aspects of your business while they're there. It may be one of the few times that you don't have to worry when Revenue Canada calls to see your records.

How Long Do I Have to File the SR&ED Forms?

To be eligible to claim SR&ED tax deductions and tax credits, you must file the form T661 on time. If you are late in filing the form T661, you will lose forever the ability to claim the tax benefits of the SR&ED expenditures for that period.

Determining when the T661 form is required to be filed is not an easy task. It used to be that you had up to ten years to file the form. Then in the February 22, 1994 budget, the government decided to dramatically reduce the time frame. This left everyone scrambling to submit claims for old SR&ED activities by September 13, 1994.

Tax Beater

File your SR&ED forms before the deadline or lose the tax benefits forever.

For taxation years commencing after 1995, the filing deadline for the T661 is twelve months after your filing due date for the year you incurred the SR&ED expenditures. Therefore, if your sole proprietorship had a January 1997 year-end, you would have until June 15, 1999, to file the T661. Your January 1997 year-end is included in your 1997 personal tax return which is due by June 15, 1998. You have up until twelve months from June 15, 1998, to file the T661.

What Happens When I Receive the Refund?

Investment tax credits must be applied to reduce your pool of SR&ED expenditures in the year after you apply for the credits. As discussed earlier, all SR&ED expenditures are placed in a pool and deducted at your discretion. If after deducting the refunded investment tax credits there is a negative balance in the pool, you will need to add the negative balance to your income.

For example, if you had SR&ED expenditures of $10,000 and you deducted $8,500 in your business, the balance of $1,500 you can carry forward in your pool. On the $10,000 of SR&ED expenditures you would have claimed an investment tax credit of $2,000. The full $2,000 investment tax credit must be applied to reduce your pool, which will leave a negative balance in the pool of $500. This negative balance of $500 must be included in your income.

This procedure is consistent with the idea that investment tax credits must be included in income or reduce a CCA class to which the tax credit relates in the year after the year you reduce your tax liability for the tax credit. However, with SR&ED investment tax credits, they reduce the SR&ED expenditure pool, which can then delay the timing of including the credits in income.

The inclusion of the investment tax credits in income is often forgotten by many taxpayers. This is especially important if you are hiring someone to review your files to submit a claim for SR&ED tax credits. Very often the fee structure for this work is based on a percentage of the investment tax refund. However, rarely is any consideration given to the tax implications of the refund. If 40% of an investment tax credit refund is paid to the firm making the claim and 50% is paid to the government in additional taxes, not much is left over for yourself.

Tax Beater

Remember that investment tax credits are included in income when hiring someone to submit your claim.

One final comment about SR&ED expenditures. This is a very complex area in tax. There are many possible ways of legitimately increasing the amount of your investment tax credits. In this Round I have tried to cover some of the more important tax aspects that you should be aware of. If you have the possibility of significant SR&ED expenditures, you should seek the assistance of a professional tax coach. The tax credits are lucrative and worth the time spent.

And the Winner Is...

Just like winning a prize fight, to "Beat the Taxman" takes know-how, determination, discipline, and a little bit of luck. The previous Rounds contain an arsenal of moves that can be used to reduce your tax liability. Some moves are simple, like paying your taxes and instalments on time. Other ideas are slightly more complex, like using corporations to defer tax or applying for scientific research and experimental development tax credits. However, they all have one thing in common: Used properly they can save you tax dollars.

Once you have the know-how, the next step is to take this information and act on it. In some cases this may require more knowledge. You may need to seek the advice of a tax coach. Or it may just require some clarification with Revenue Canada on the application of the rules to your particular business. Either way, if in doubt seek additional knowledge and expert advice.

Once you are sure that the idea applies to you and your business, it will take determination on your part to ensure that the tax savings will occur. This may mean a change in the way you do things. Maybe this will mean recording the business transactions more frequently. Maybe you will have to procrastinate less and get documents filed on time. Maybe you will need to sit down with your banker and discuss ways to finance your business to ensure you are maximizing your tax deductions. Whatever the changes may be, you will need to be determined in your approach.

But determination alone is not enough. Just because you are determined to win the fight, doesn't necessarily mean you will. You also need to be disciplined. I am not talking about an onerous kind of discipline that will require all of your focus and concentration. Instead, I simply refer to a tax-savings discipline: A conscious intention to conduct your business in a manner that will maximize your tax savings and business profits. When these two ideals clash, you must choose which is more important. But the key is remembering that significant tax saving occurs through a disciplined approach throughout the year. You don't train for a fight in one day. Similarly you don't save taxes one day of the year.

And finally, I wish you the best of luck in your business endeavours and your tax savings fight.

Quick Reference to Tax Beaters

1. Deduct the cost of this book and save.

2. Report all legitimate business expenses even if you incur persistent losses.

3. Record all business-related expenses between startup and your first sale.

4. Don't spend money on your business before official startup.

5. The general rule: all reasonable business-related expenses are tax deductible.

6. Know and follow the rules for self-employment.

7. Record all expenses to save tax dollars.

8. Accurate records can help you prove your case to Revenue Canada.

9. Even without a receipt you can still claim an expense.

10. Where no description shows on a receipt, itemize the purchase yourself.

11. Record your transactions weekly so you don't forget a business expense.

12. Use a double-entry record-keeping system to avoid costly mistakes.

13. By timing purchases and sales at year-end, the cash method can save you tax.

14. Defer tax by staying with a non-December year-end if your income is increasing.

15. Save tax by changing to a December year-end if income from an established business is decreasing.

16. Elect to include income in your first year of business to reduce income taxed at high tax rates.

17. Elect to defer income that will be taxed in the current year at the highest tax rate.

18. Choose a December year-end if your new business is losing money.

19. Maximize income in lower tax levels and minimize income in higher tax levels.

20. Save significant tax dollars by legally allocating income among family members.

21. Lending money to a family member to finance a small or home-based business is allowable income splitting.

22. Save as much as $3,400 per child, per year, by putting your children on salary.

23. Pay a dependent parent a salary.

24. If your income is in excess of $29,590 and your spouse is in a lower bracket, pay your spouse a salary.

25. Salary for family members must be reasonable and for services rendered.

26. Apply to have your family member EI exempt.

27. Apply for refunds of EI paid to family members for up to three prior years.

28. If you do not already have employees, consider making your family member(s) partners. This avoids costs and headaches involved in having a payroll.

29. Make spousal RRSP contributions to save taxes today and tomorrow.

30. Hold off deducting your RRSP contribution in a year where your income is low and you expect next year's income to be high.

31. Claim business losses on your tax return to receive an immediate tax refund or reduce future tax liabilities.

32. File loss carry-back election on time in order to get your refund.

33. Apply a loss to the third prior taxation year before it is too late.

34. Apply a loss over the past three years to minimize higher income levels.

35. Carry losses forward if next year's income is expected to be high.

36. Claim a reserve for income that has been received but in return for services which have not been rendered or goods have not been shipped.

37. Claim reserves on questionable receivables.

38. Defer claiming CCA on fast write-off assets in low income years to get more dollar for your deduction.

39. Highly successful small-business entrepreneurs should consider using a corporation to defer up to $68,000 a year in taxes.

40. Save time and money by choosing the proper business structure.

41. To save money and avoid hassles, develop a partnership agreement.

42. Save taxes in start-up years where you have losses by using the sole proprietorship or partnership structure.

43. Defer up to 28% in taxes by using a corporation properly.

44. Save thousands of dollars by selling shares that qualify for the $500,000 capital gains exemption.

45. Save taxes by transferring profitable businesses into a corporation and keeping losing businesses as sole proprietorships.

46. Register for GST if you are selling zero-rated goods and services to obtain refund of GST on purchases.

47. Register for the GST and increase profits.

48. Register for the GST at start up and claim input tax credits on all your business purchases.

49. Reduce tax and simplify GST record-keeping by using the "Quick Method."

50. Maximize your GST savings by claiming the 1% reduction.

51. Remember to claim input tax credits on capital purchases when using the "Quick Method."

52. Claim forgotten input tax credits before the four-year limitation is up.

53. Request GST information be included on purchase invoices to save money and hassles.

54. Remember to include input tax credits on capital purchases used in your business.

55. Claim Input Tax Credits on personal capital property used more than 50% of the time in your taxable business.

56. Claim Input Tax Credits on general operating expenses for items used more than 10% of the time in a taxable business.

57. Speed up Input Tax Credit refunds by electing to file quarterly or monthly.

58. Reduce hassles and reporting costs by filing GST returns only as required.

59. Remit your GST on time.

60. Remember to request a refund of the GST and PST on accounts receivable that you have written off.

61. Remember to charge GST on the sale of used capital assets or you will be paying the tax out of your pocket.

62. Don't forget to charge and remit the GST on the trade-in of business vehicles or you will be liable for the GST.

63. File your tax return and pay any balance owing by April 30 to avoid being charged interest.

64. Reduce the money you pay the government by paying and filing your tax return on time.

65. Pay your tax instalments as required to reduce your overall costs and increase profits.

66. Follow the "No-Calculation Option" when your income is stable or rising to minimize the amount of pre-paid tax.

67. Increase cash flow by electing to use alternative instalment options.

68. Use the "Current-Year Instalment Option" in years of declining income to maximize cash flow and personal wealth.

69. If you miss an instalment payment, catch up your instalments and prepay the next instalment to reduce or eliminate the non-deductible instalment interest charge.

70. Properly withhold and remit payroll taxes on time.

71. Increase cash flow and save time by electing to reduce your payroll remittance frequency.

72. Reduce the sting of infractions by knowing which fines and penalties are tax-deductible.

73. Turn personal loans into business loans and deduct the interest for tax purposes.

74. Pay down personal loans before business loans to maximize your tax deductible interest expense.

75. Structure business loans to turn non-deductible insurance

premiums into tax-deductible expenditures.

76. Maximize your tax savings on course fees by taking those courses that are fully deductible for income tax purposes.

77. Know which conventions are tax deductible and attend accordingly.

78. When advertising to the Canadian public, advertise with Canadian media to ensure your advertising dollars are tax deductible.

79. Reduce taxes by not including in your year-end inventory, obsolete or damaged goods.

80. Provide for doubtful paying customers and defer tax dollars.

81. Consider requesting Revenue Canada to reverse interest and penalties.

82. If your home is not your principal place of business, designate an area in your home to be used solely for business purposes and conduct client meetings at home.

83. If your home is your principal place of business, maximize your tax deductions by designating an area in your home to be used exclusively for your business.

84. Maximize the home area used in your business or minimize the area of your home.

85. New or increased home costs that are a direct result of your business can be deducted 100% as a business expense.

86. A separate telephone line for your business is 100% tax deductible.

87. Keep track of the business portion of home expenses so each year you can deduct them either in the current year or in a profitable year.

88. Maximize your tax savings by properly classifying the business portion of home expenses from business expenses.

89. Maximize tax savings by knowing the difference between

a capital and an expense purchase.

90. Claim full depreciation on assets not subject to the half-rate rule.

91. Claim terminal losses to maximize your tax savings.

92. Delay claiming CCA in times where you may lose the use of the deduction.

93. When deferring CCA deductions, start by deferring fast-depreciating assets first to provide maximum flexibility.

94. Purchase assets at the end of the business year instead of the beginning of the next year.

95. Ensure that your capital purchase is available-for-use by the end of your business year, even if you don't, in fact, use it.

96. If near your year-end, delay the sale of a capital asset until early the next year.

97. When purchasing a computer and software at the same time, break out the software portion of the purchase and deduct at the 100% CCA rate.

98. Elect to include electronic office equipment in a separate CCA class to potentially increase your tax deductions on sale.

99. Deduct 100% of the cost of tools costing less than $200.

100. Deduct CCA on personal assets which are now being used in your business.

101. Deduct a portion of the cost of assets used both personally and in a business.

102. Consider late-filing the $100,000 capital gains election on built-up goodwill. You could save thousands of dollars.

103. Record all business kilometres you drive.

104. Keep all automotive receipts to support your tax deduction.

105. If two or more vehicles are used in your business, keep track of the business kilometres on each vehicle to

maximize your tax deductions.

106. Maximize tax savings by using the vehicle with higher operating costs.

107. Record your odometer readings at the beginning and end of each year.

108. Schedule client meetings on the way to and from work to increase business kilometres and save taxes.

109. Avoid class 10.1 restrictions by negotiating favourable new vehicle purchase deals.

110. Maximize your lease deduction by keeping operating expenses out of the lease agreement.

111. Arrange new car financing so that none of the interest is restricted.

112. Own your personal vehicle personally instead of in a corporation.

113. When personal kilometres are low, use the 12 cents per personal kilometre method of calculating your operating taxable benefit.

114. Before purchasing your vehicle, compare the standby charge under the lease option.

115. Reduce your standby charge by selling your vehicle to one of your other operating companies.

116. Save time and money: pay yourself a reasonable tax-free car allowance on personally owned vehicles.

117. Reduce the tax you pay with investment tax credits.

118. Amend prior year tax returns to save on forgotten investment tax credits.

119. Apply for 40% investment tax credit refund to speed up tax savings.

120. Apply unused investment tax credits to past and future taxation years.

121. Reduce CCA claims to use up investment tax credits before they expire.

122. File your tax return on time to ensure ITC carry backs are accepted by Revenue Canada.

123. Delay deducting SR&ED expenses to reduce risk of loss carry forwards expiring.

124. Deduct SR&ED capital expenditures all in one year.

125. Consider incorporating your business to receive an additional 15% investment tax credit.

126. Claim your 40% refund of excess investment tax credits on your personal return.

127. Consider incorporating your business to receive a 100% refund of investment tax credits.

128. File your SR&ED forms before the deadline or lose the tax benefits forever.

129. Remember that investment tax credits are included in income when hiring someone to submit your claim.

Appendix

Statement of Business Income and Loss
For The Period (enter beginning and ending dates)
(The following schedule has been designed to closely resemble Revenue
Canada's form T2124, Statement of Business Activities)

		$	$
Income			
Sales income—net of GST/PST and returns, allowances			———
Reserves deducted last year			———
Other income			———
Gross income (total of above three lines)	a		———
Calculation of cost of goods sold			
Opening inventory (include raw materials, goods in process, and finished goods)		———	
Purchases during the year (net of returns, allowances, and discounts)		———	
Sub-contracts		———	
Direct wage costs		———	
Other costs		———	
Total of above five lines		———	
Minus – Closing inventory (include raw materials, goods in process, and finished goods)		———	
Cost of goods sold	b		———
Gross Profit (line a minus line b)	c		———

	$	$
Business Expenses		
Advertising	————	
Bad debts	————	
Business tax, fees, licences, dues, memberships, and subscriptions	————	
Delivery, freight and express	————	
Fuel costs (except for motor vehicles)	————	
Insurance (other than for the home)	————	
Interest (other than for the home mortgage)	————	
Maintenance and repairs (other than for the home or vehicle)	————	
Meals and entertainment (50% only - except in Quebec)	————	
Motor vehicle expenses (not including capital cost allowance)	————	
Office expenses	————	
Supplies	————	
Legal, accounting, and other professional fees	————	
Property taxes (other than for the home)	————	
Rent (other than for the home)	————	
Salaries, wages, and benefits (including employer's contributions)	————	
Travel	————	
Telephone	————	
Utilities (other than for the home)	————	
Other expenses	————	
Capital cost allowance	————	
Allowance on eligible capital property	————	
Total business expenses d		————
Net income (loss) before adjustments (line c minus line d) e		————

Adjustments to Net Income (Loss)
For the Period (enter beginning and ending dates)

$

Net income (loss) before adjustments (line e from previous page)   f   —————

Your share of line f (include on this line your share of the income or loss.

   If you are in a partnership, include your share of the partnership income

   or loss.)   g   —————

Minus other amounts deductible from your share of the net partnership

   income (loss) (attach list)   h   —————

Net income (loss) after adjustments (line g minus line h)   i   —————

Minus business-use-of-home expenses (from m below)   j   —————

Net income (loss) (line i minus line j)   —————

Calculation of Business-Use-Of-Home Expenses

Heat   —————

Electricity   —————

Insurance   —————

Mortgage interest   —————

Property taxes   —————

Other expenses   —————

   Subtotal   —————

Minus personal use portion   —————

   Subtotal   —————

Plus amount carried forward from previous year   —————

   Subtotal   k   —————

Minus net income (loss) after adjustments from line i above (if negative,

   enter "0")   l   —————

Business-use-of-home expenses available for carry forward (line k minus line l)

   if negative, enter "0"   —————

Allowable claim (the lower of amounts on line k or on line l) enter this

   amount on line j above   m   —————

Typical Small Business Capital Expenditures
Complete With CCA Class and CCA Rate

Asset Description	CCA Class	CCA Rate
Automobile-passenger vehicle costing < $24,000 or a non-passenger vehicle	10	30%
Automobile-passenger vehicle costing > $24,000	10.1	30%
Automotive equipment	10	30%
Billboards, acquired after 1987	8	20%
Buildings-brick, stone, cement, etc., acquired after 1987	1	4%
Buildings-frame, log, stucco on frame, galvanized iron or corrugated metal if unsupported below ground subject to certain restrictions	6	10%
Calculator	8	20%
Chinaware and cutlery[2]	12	100%
Computer[1]	10	30%
Computer software	12	100%
Costumes and accessories for earning rental income[2]	12	100%
Cutting part of a machine	12	100%
Dental instruments (costing less than $200)[2]	12	100%
Desk	8	20%
Dies	12	100%
Electrical advertising signs	8	20%
Fax machine[1]	8	20%
Fences	6	10%
Filing cabinet	8	20%
Furniture and equipment not included in any other class	8	20%
Glass tableware[2]	12	100%
Land	N/A	Nil
Linen[2]	12	100%
Machinery and equipment not specifically listed	8	20%

Asset Description	CCA Class	CCA Rate
Machinery and equipment used primarily in manufacturing and processing (acquired after February 25, 1992)	43	30%
Medical equipment (costing less than $200)[2]	12	100%
Metric scales	8	20%
Outdoor advertising billboards acquired after 1987	8	20%
Parking area	17	8%
Radio communication equipment	8	20%
Refrigeration equipment	8	20%
Sidewalks	17	8%
Small tools (costing less than $200)[2]	12	100%
Taxicabs	16	40%
Telegraph and telephone equipment	8	20%
Tile drainage - other than for farmers	8	20%
Tractors for hauling freight	16	40%
Trucks, automotive (unless passenger vehicle costing > $24,000)	10	30%
Trucks, for hauling freight	16	40%
Uniforms[2]	12	100%
Video games	8	20%
Video games (coin-operated)	16	40%
Video tapes for lease	12	100%

[1] See Round 9 for more details on how to save tax dollars with the purchase of electronic office equipment.

[2] The half rate rule does not apply to this asset. The full cost of the asset may be written off in the first year.

Index

Subscribe Today
to

Beat the Taxman!

NEWSLETTER

**CANADA'S TAX-SAVING NEWSLETTER
FOR SMALL-BUSINESS ENTREPRENEURS**

Stephen Thompson's *Beat the Taxman! Newsletter* provides you with up-to-date insights that are designed to maximize the savings you will earn through conscientious and aggressive (but very legal!!) tax planning. This newsletter has been created to furnish you with the best available tax-saving tips and techniques. It is filled with practical advice, the latest research, upcoming trends, and brand new tax-saving strategies—all designed to pay off on your bottom line.

Every new subscriber to the *Beat the Taxman! Newsletter* is given this unique guarantee: Examine your first issue for 21 days. If you aren't convinced that the newsletter will save you taxes, your subscription fee will be refunded—no questions asked.

To subscribe simply call or fax the attached order form to:

STEPHEN THOMPSON, CA
Wilkinson & Company
Chartered Accountants
Tax-Savings Specialists for Successful Entrepreneurs
71 Dundas Street West
P.O. Box 400
Trenton, Ontario, K8V 5R6
Telephone: 613-392-2592 or 1-888-713-SAVE
Fax: 613-392-8512   Email: stevet@wilkinson.reach.net

YES! I'd like to save tax by subscribing to the
Beat the Taxman! Newsletter

Name: _____

Address: _____

_____

_____

Company: _____

Phone: _____ Fax: _____

☐   Annual Subscription Fee $60 + 4.20 (GST) = $64.20
(4 issues)

☐   Two-Year Subscription Fee $110 + 7.70 (GST) = $117.70
(8 issues)

☐   Cheque enclosed

or charge my   VISA ☐   MASTERCARD ☐

Card No. _____

Expiry Date: _____

Signature: _____